DECIPHERING
CHINA'S
MICR⬛CHIP
INDUSTRY

DECIPHERING CHINA'S MICROCHIP INDUSTRY

CHEN Fang
DONG Ruifeng

World Scientific

NEW JERSEY · LONDON · SINGAPORE · BEIJING · SHANGHAI · HONG KONG · TAIPEI · CHENNAI · TOKYO

Published by

World Scientific Publishing Co. Pte. Ltd.

5 Toh Tuck Link, Singapore 596224

USA office: 27 Warren Street, Suite 401-402, Hackensack, NJ 07601

UK office: 57 Shelton Street, Covent Garden, London WC2H 9HE

Library of Congress Cataloging-in-Publication Data

Names: Chen, Fang (Reporter), author. | Dong, Ruifeng, author.

Title: Deciphering China's microchip industry / CHEN Fang, DONG Ruifeng.

Description: Singapore ; Hackensack, NJ : World Scientific, [2020] |
    Includes bibliographical references.

Identifiers: LCCN 2020013216 | ISBN 9789811217210 (hardback) |
    ISBN 9789811218415 (paperback) | ISBN 9789811217227 (ebook for institutions) |
    ISBN 9789811217234 (ebook for individuals)

Subjects: LCSH: Integrated circuits industry--China.

Classification: LCC HD9696.I583 C644 2020 | DDC 338.4/762138150951--dc23

LC record available at https://lccn.loc.gov/2020013216

British Library Cataloguing-in-Publication Data

A catalogue record for this book is available from the British Library.

"芯"想事成: 中国芯片产业的博弈与突围

Originally published in Chinese by Posts and Telecom Press

Copyright © Posts & Telecom Press 2018

For any available supplementary material, please visit
https://www.worldscientific.com/worldscibooks/10.1142/11745#t=suppl

Desk Editor: Dong Lixi

Typeset by Stallion Press

Email: enquiries@stallionpress.com

Contents

About the Authors

CHEN Fang is a senior reporter at Xinhua News Agency and a winner of the "Top Ten Editors" laurel. Chen has been engaged in reporting about macro-economy, science and technology events for a long time, and is dedicated to the investigation and research of major and focal issues. Many of Chen's works have earned her awards in Chinese journalism.

DONG Ruifeng is a Chief reporter at Xinhua News Agency. Dong has been engaged in current affairs reporting for a long time. He focuses on writing scientific and technological reports. Many of Dong's works have won him China Science and Technology Good News Award.

Preface

The survival race looming in China's semiconductor industry is becoming ever so nerve-racking and gut-wrenching.

On 16th April 2018, the United States Department of Commerce (DOC) launched a 7-year export restriction on ZTE Corporation, banning US suppliers from selling high-tech components and software products to the Chinese company. The news startled China. Even journalists who had been closely tracking technology events were surprised that the US government would target a Chinese enterprise and that China's second largest as well as the world's fourth largest telecoms company could be devastated by this sudden attack.

From the "301 investigation" to the extra tariffs list to an all-round export restriction on core semiconductor components, the US is turning up the heat in its confrontation with China.

There are more than one signs that showed that the ZTE incident is not an isolated happening, and China's semiconductor industry is not the only pressure point in this power game. Instead, it is just one punch among a series of well-designed attacks, or one move in a scheming chess game. All of these deserve a scrutiny from both a historical angle and a macro, global perspective.

Microchips are the cornerstone of the modern industrial and information society, the core technology of which is so pivotal in a country's sustainable leadership that no ambitious country can afford to be locked in a cut throat competition.

China's information technology (IT) industry has been on an exponential rise for the past several decades. However, its semiconductor industry, especially in the core and advanced fields, has not seen a substantial progress which could enable it to compete on a par with the world's leading players. China's behindhand in semiconductors has been for a long time a typical "Gray Rhino" neglected by many.

In the global arena today, independence and controllability of core technologies has become a major strategic concern when it comes to national security. It is high time for China's microchip companies to stop the old practice of following the footsteps of others.

However, should they devote time, energy and money into developing core technologies which have long been dominated by the West? How can they balance the pursuit of technology and the demands of market to make valuable and profitable products? What stories and lessons are behind China's semiconductor industry being blocked by the US ? These questions are what we will bear in mind as we delve into the history of China's semiconductor development, and we will find them existent and explored even back then.

China is well aware of the strategic significance of semiconductors in both domestic development and international competition. It has tried to draw lessons from America's practice of market competition, Japan's innovation of industrial guidance and Korea's success of capital support, but to replicate prosperity in a different country at a different time seems to be not very promising.

Many would think that China's semiconductor industry has missed the golden age of industrial development in the latter half of the last century, therefore it is natural and necessary for the newcomer to climb more and higher mountains within a shorter period of time in order to catch up with the forerunners. Sometimes, unusual strategies and approaches are necessary. For example, China's Ark, Loongson and Sunway have proved that mastering core technologies to build up competitiveness is a long-term process of accumulation, which demands patience, perseverance and big investments.

Others think that the ZTE incident is an acid test for China's science and technology industry and that China is exposed as untenable under such a test. However, it is rather rash and risky to take such a polarized and prejudiced stand. It is true that China has a long way to go compared with other science and technology powers in the world, but at the same time, the potential it presents is also admittedly remarkable.

What's more, innovation has always been a trial and error process that requires constant design and redesign, thinking and rethinking. Only through careful selection of markets and learning from mistakes can products be improved and technology be optimized.

After the ZTE incident, China's leading scientists and entrepreneurs, many of whom had never or seldom made any public appearances, chose to come together and voice out about the significance and difficulty of realizing scientific and technological independence and controllability. They believed that while China is being challenged, it is also prepared for the fight, and that the road of thorns it faces ahead is also a road of roses. They urged for more opportunities and allowances for trial and error in China's domestic microchips enterprises.

In this book, we endeavor to find the answers to questions such as: What is behind the US-China trade friction, or "war" as many have chosen to call it, as the whole episode evolves toward an aggravated level? Why is China's microchips industry caught in such a dilemma? Where does the future lies and where will it all lead to?

It is not an easy task to choose and select from an ocean of raw materials about China's and the world's semiconductors development history, and to rearrange them into an understandable and even enjoyable event map that could work to answer the above questions.

We owe a great debt to many friends and colleagues for their continued assistance and encouragement.

The Posts and Telecom Press, besides providing background support for this project, took pains to critically read parts of our manuscript. Without their patience and proficiency, we would never be able to complete this book in just a few months.

Our acknowledgment also goes to our colleagues at the Xinhua News Agency: Cai Mingzhao, the General Director of the agency; He Ping, the General Editor; Liu Siyang, Zhang Sutang and Yan Wenbin, our three Vice Directors; Zhao Chen, Qin Jie, Chen Wanjuan, Huo

Xiaoguang and Chen Er'hou, our colleagues from the agency's domestic department. They are our tutors as well as companions in our quest for truth and the essence behind the truth.

We are also indebted to our families for their unconditional support in order for us to dedicate such a large proportion of our spare time to this book.

Just as we were going to give this book the finishing touch, news came across the Pacific Ocean that on 13th July 2018, the DOC lifted the export restriction on ZTE. After three months of disturbing uncertainty, the ZTE incident finally reached its turning point.

Meanwhile, the world had been as evolving and uncertain as ever during these three months. The US threatened to impose extra tariffs on US$500 billion of Chinese goods, up from the previous US$50 billion; the EU slapped a record-high fine on Google, signaling a downturn of US-Europe trade relations; the US President and the Russian President finally met but reached no substantial progress; Japan and the EU struck an initial agreement to establish the world's biggest free trade zone.

After all these ups and downs, there are some things that have been essentially altered. Science and technology are witnessing an unprecedented revolution and the global economic system is yearning for a fundamental readjustment. No one can deny that this is the start of a massive transformation.

And microchips, the size of a fingernail, is standing at the forefront of this impending sea change.

We hereby heartily dedicate this book to all who wish to feel the pulse of this era.

Chen Fang & Dong Ruifeng
July 2018

Chapter 1

The US Wants a High-tech Cold War?

Overture

Trade relations between the US and China are increasingly fraught with tension.

The value of goods upon which excessive tariffs have been imposed jumps from US$50 billion to a threatening US$200 billion and then to an astonishing US$500 billion; the trade relation between the US and China plummets from the sizzling frying pan to the blazing fire.

Like a huge rock thrown into a calm lake, the billowing waves are warnings that the "Gray Rhino" is gathering speed and coming right at the Chinese high-tech sector.

This is going to be a high-tech race indeed. The two racers, however, are not at the same starting line. The frontrunner decides to use its dominance to maintain its lead, while the newcomer is using all its might to establish its own strength.

The fate of the world cannot be foretold and drastic changes can take place in the blink of an eye; just like the lightning rod, calm and still this second, and churning with concentrating and intensifying electrons far and near the next second.

Will ZTE make it through this turbulent storm?

> **The night is long that never finds the day.**
> **— William Shakespeare, *Macbeth***

1.1 A Takedown from the US

On 20th January 2017 at 12 p.m. local time on the West Front of the United States Capitol Building in Washington, D. C., 71-year-old billionaire businessman Donald Trump was sworn in as the 45th President of the United States under the witness and applause of an estimated 150,000 attendees.

The newly elected US President Donald Trump giving his inauguration speech.

One thousand nine hundred kilometers away in Richardson, Texas, the President's inauguration was telecast live on every television screen in ZTE's US headquarter building. Ripples of uneasiness passed through Cheng Lixin, the director of ZTE US. The new President, who stormed his way into the White House proclaiming America First with an unabashed attitude, was known for not playing by the rules in his co-authored book, *Trump: The Art of the Deal*.

In the city of Richardson, within a locality of no more than 73 square kilometers and about 100,000 residents, there were more than 5,000 IT companies of various sizes, including leading ones like

AT&T, Ericsson, Cisco, Samsung, Texas Instruments and Fujitsu. In this community inhabited by a large number of high-tech players, ZTE was the new kid on the block.

Like other foreign enterprises in the US who were prepared to go the extra mile to blend in with their American surroundings, ZTE sponsored several Texas-based National Basketball Association teams, hired top-of-the-crop law firms and lobbying firms to help it hold its ground and gave US$3 to 5 billion each year in exchange for licenses to certain technologies and top-notch chips patented by US companies. Despite all these, it seemed that the Chinese new arrival and the US watchdog did not succeed in getting along with each other.

In 2012, the United States House of Committee issued a report on the national security implications of Huawei and ZTE, two of China's largest telecoms company. However, it did not manage to acquire clear-cut facts and provide positive proof to pin down the two companies based on the panel's verdict of "untrustworthiness". In 2016, the US DOC accused ZTE of violating US economic sanctions on Iran and North Korea. The company faced an export restriction by the US government, that is, US component makers were prohibited from supplying ZTE with their parts, including chips used in its telecoms equipment and mobile devices.

The company was unsurprisingly on good terms with a handful of US suppliers. As one of the world's leading providers of structured telecommunications solutions, ZTE had been providing services for hundreds of thousands of high-tech jobs in the US. It would suffice to say that for a company with a business network covering more than 150 countries and a global human resource pool of more than 80,000 people, normal business setbacks could do little to knock it over. On the contrary, these stumbling blocks would only serve to make ZTE stronger by pushing it to confront and rise above these inevitable bumps along the way. It was true. Instead of being on tenterhooks after being labeled as untrustworthy by the US House Committee, ZTE used the opportunity to launch a new series of commercial ads and to showcase its corporate social responsibility by throwing charity parties with the likes of the famous Huston Rockets. As Cheng said in a press interview, "The speculated accusation in the report has failed to diminish ZTE's commercial activities in the United States... This unexpected episode actually lends itself well to the management of our brand image."

When Trump was inaugurated as the new President of the United States, ZTE's negotiations with the DOC was in the stage of approaching an agreement. Two months later, after the Chinese telecoms giant agreed to pay a penalty of US$8,900 million, it was allowed to continue to work with its US suppliers under certain rules laid out in the agreement. Although it was a huge fine, for a company with an annual turnover of US$15 billion, this blow was not too severe to take.

The day before Trump's inauguration, Cheng posted several photos of the White House onto his Weibo (China's Facebook) account, and wrote, "The USA is ready for the new President". Never did he nor board members at ZTE's Chinese headquarters in Shenzhen, Guangdong imagine that the new President was about to exert his art of the deal and push them over a sharp cliff one year later.

On 15th April 2018, the DOC re-launched the export restriction on ZTE and set it in motion without warning. A seven-year restriction that would ban US suppliers from selling high-tech components and software products to ZTE was put into action right away. The restriction was supposed to be suspended according to the agreement reached one year ago, but it was triggered by the DOC and completely blindsided ZTE. The ban would be effective till 13th March 2025.

Accompanying the DOC's announcement was news of ZTE's US suppliers tearing up their supply contracts with the company. An insider from ZTE was quoted as saying that they were prohibited from making any contact with personnel in their US business partners such as Qualcomm, Intel and Broadcom.

The *Financial Times* commented that this action effectively banned all US companies from doing business with China's second largest telecoms company all over the world.

The electronics giant was being cornered to the brink of collapse. However, how did this saga even come about?

It is estimated that ZTE purchases about 2,000 million chips each year from US semiconductor producers including Intel, Qualcomm, Xilinx, Texas Instruments and Analog Devices. US companies are also believed to have provided more than a quarter of the components used in ZTE telecoms equipment and mobile devices. The real debacle, however, is the inability of Chinese firms to fill the gap when foreign supplies are restricted. When the US activated the export restriction on 15th April 2018, ZTE hit a dead end because its assembly lines could not scrape by for even two months without US-made components and chips.

On the same day, trading in ZTE shares were suspended in both the Shenzhen Stock Exchange and the Hong Kong Stock Exchange. The *Forbes* magazine gloomily predicted that the cornered Chinese company was likely to file for bankruptcy within a few weeks.

Before this catastrophic storm swept through, ZTE was embracing its best financial year ever, with an operation revenue of 108.82 billion yuan (US$16.24 billion, a 7.5% year-on-year growth) and a net profit attributable to listed shareholders of 4.57 billion yuan (US$682 million, a 293.8% year-on-year growth). 2018 could have been another encouraging year, which witnessed ZTE gaining ground on the commercial deployment of 5G networks. What was ahead of ZTE should have been prosperity rather than teeth-clenching frustration.

The outlook was bleak and it was spiraling down relentlessly. On the morning of 20th April, ZTE posted an official statement to protest and condemn the decision of the US Bureau of Industry and Security (BIS) as unfair and irresponsible, as the harshest sanction was imposed even before relevant investigations entered its final leg. On the same day in the afternoon, the company's CEO Yin Yimin admitted outright in a press conference held at the Shenzhen headquarters that the US ban would likely cause ZTE to suffer a shock.

ZTE's press conference held at its Shenzhen headquarters right after the US ban.

1.2 Why ZTE?

As a company that pioneered the globalization process of Chinese telecoms firms, ZTE is no doubt a success and a role-model. The marathon runner in the global telecoms industry has achieved global expansion through hard work in science and technology innovations as well as international market operations.

This successful company is one of the world's four largest telecommunications equipment manufacturers; it boasts a top three ranking in global Patent Cooperation Treaty (PCT) applications for 8 consecutive years and is a model enterprise for Chinese high-tech companies expanding overseas. Having achieved all these accolades, it would be hard to understand how the giant is pushed to the edge by the US government.

1. *ZTE Enters the Global 5G Battlefield*

Many believed that the United States' real purpose behind its attack on China's two largest telecoms firms is to force China to the bargaining table and put a lid on its 5G development.

5G, aka 5th generation wireless technology, has been under the global spotlight and receiving unprecedented attention. Unlike its predecessors like 2G, 3G and 4G technologies, which developed mainly under industrial and commercial forces, 5G is in many country's national agendas that are promoting innovation-stimulating policies and investing billions of dollars to the research and development of the future-defining technology.

The US is starting to lose its upper hand in the 3G and 4G industries, and to lose its edge in the important 5G competition arena would be the last thing it wants. In fact, it is planning to take the absolute lead. In July 2016, the United States Federal Communications Committee allocated frequency bands for 5G network construction, making the US the first nation in the world to allot 5G frequency resources. Wilbur Ross, the US Secretary of Commerce, said that America's 5G development should be a priority for the Trump administration.

At the same time, America's three largest telecoms carriers, Verizon, AT&T and T-Mobile announced their 5G programs and started to experiment on some key technologies and commercial deployments together with electronic giants including Samsung, Ericsson, Nokia, Qualcomm and Intel. It was estimated that they would be able to bring 5G technology into commercial application as early as 2018.

Chinese players are featured on the 5G stage as well, as represented by two active and promising participants, Huawei and ZTE, who has never before in history been so close to the center stage of a new thrilling technology. In the last two years, ZTE had been expanding its services and businesses for its 5G deployment — taking up 13% of global market share for telecoms equipment, showing up at fourth place in the US mobile market share, investing more than 12% of its revenue into R&D, offering end-to-end solutions that covered the entire telecommunications domain for more than 150 countries and areas, and establishing an advanced service package for global network delivery, operation and maintenance. By the end of 2017, ZTE had more than 2,000 patents on 5G technology.

It was on this upswing when ZTE was targeted by the US government.

The founder of ZTE, Hou Weigui.

Thirty-five years ago in August 1984 in China, Hou Weigui, then the technology director of a plant for aeronautical and space use, was in the newly opened special economic zone of Shenzhen, with an assigned duty to search for a partner to start something new. Nine months later, a company named Zhongxing was set up in Shenzhen. Its name, Zhongxing (中兴), literally translated as "China prospers". With a registered capital of 2.8 million yuan and Hou at the helm, it was about to march into the semiconductor industry.

That was the very beginning of the long journey taken by Zhongxing, now ZTE. Five years after it was born, Zhongxing successfully developed the first digital SPC switch with its own independent intellectual property rights, morphing into a telecommunications equipment manufacturer from an unnoteworthy maker of digital watches, electric fans and telephones. Another eight years later, the same year when Hong Kong was handed back to China, Zhongxing was listed in the Shenzhen Stock Exchange with a new name, Zhongxing Telecommunications Equipment (ZTE). Following that, it became the first A-shares company to be listed in the Hong Kong Stock Exchange.

The year 2007 was another milestone in ZTE's history, which witnessed its global sales volume climbing to eighth place among established telecoms companies such as Ericsson and Nokia. By the time long-serving steersman Hou passed the helm to Yin, ZTE had already become an international telecoms giant with a hundreds-of-billions-yuan sales volume, 8,000 employees and a business empire spanning from telecoms equipment, mobile phones to computer hardware and software.

2. *The ZTE Saga*

In 2012, ZTE sold products that contained software and hardware produced by US IT companies to the Iranian telecoms carrier through contracted deals. The transaction might have violated the US' *Iranian Transactions and Sanctions Regulations (ITSR)*, which stated that any form of selling any US-origin high-tech products to Iran was deemed as illegal.

Reuters exposed the deal and the FBI began to carry out an all-round investigation into ZTE's background and activities. Results were announced four years later by the DOC, which verified ZTE's violation on ITSR, resulting in an export restriction on the Chinese company. The DOC also published on its website some of ZTE's internal documents which showed that the company's Iranian programs did depend to a certain extent on US supply chains. ZTE had no other choice but to reap what it sowed.

After a year of negotiation, the Chinese firm and the US government entered into a settlement agreement which was to suspend the export restriction on the former. As per the suspension terms, ZTE was expected to plead guilty to three of the accusations made by the US government, pay US$8,900 million of penalty and fines, dismiss four top-management employees and punish another 35 workers by cutting their bonuses. In other words, in what way and how long the suspension would be carried out would be dependent on how far the company could fulfill the above terms.

It seemed that the US government was not satisfied with ZTE's performance on the suspension terms, especially as the Chinese company did not impose a punishment on those 35 employees as severely as agreed. On 13th March 2018, the BIS informed ZTE that the suspended sanction, namely the export restriction, was to be activated immediately in view of the company's violation of the suspension terms laid out in the two parties' settlement agreement. The violation was confirmed as mainly concerning the bonus issue. It was thus not a surprise that many Chinese jeered at and deplored the activation order as a punishment for giving employees bonuses.

The DOC said in its statement that ZTE failed to abide by the probationary conditions and repeatedly made false or misleading statements during the course of BIS' investigation in relation to employee discipline actions the company said it was taking or had already taken, which covered up the fact that ZTE paid full bonuses to the 35 employees who were subject to a bonus punishment as agreed in the probationary terms.

ZTE protested in its statement that the DOC ignored the fact that the bonus issue was found out by the company's own law firm and had been immediately reported to the DOC to seek mutual solutions, that relevant responsible personnel were dismissed right upon the company's discovery of the violation on the bonus rule, and that during the past two years, from when they were caught conspiring against ITSR, the company had kept a successful track record of its compliance with the Export Administration Regulation (EAR).

This twist in the saga triggered heated discussion and reaction on China's internet. Some expressed their understanding of the US' action of withdrawing ZTE's export privilege because violation was supposed to come with a price, while others argued that the bonus issue was just a trigger for America's bigger plan of stirring things up in the Chinese telecoms industry. The fate of ZTE was a card in Trump's hand when dealing with China and it could be played anytime as and when the US liked it to be. The trade tensions between the two countries after Trump came into power were the perfect opportunity to play this card.

It should be noted that before 2017, most of the trade friction initiated by the US against China concentrated on medium-to-low-end industries like steel, aluminum and photovoltaic products. In contrast, the 2018 "301 investigation" started to shift the US' target towards China's high-tech industries, with 5G at the center of this round of attack.

Behind all these moves, there is only one motive. The US needs to guarantee its leading role in science and technology development, but if China grows too fast, transitions smoothly from a labor-intensive economy to a capital-intensive one, and graduates successfully from downstream to upstream in the manufacturing value chain, then the US would be losing some (or lots of) advantages.

A recap of the ZTE saga.

Time	Events and progress
Mar. 2012	FBI formed a special committee to start the investigation on ZTE.
2014–2016	A long communication and negotiation process between ZTE and the US government.
Mar. 2016	On the 7th, the US DOC decided to put a sanction on ZTE that restricted US firm from selling core components to the latter. On the 24th, the DOC granted a temporary suspension on the sanction, which repeated several times and would last till 29th March 2017.
Jan. 2017	On the 6th, President Barack Obama's Council of Advisors on Science and Technology published a report, *Ensuring Long-term US Leadership in Semiconductors*.
Mar. 2017	A settlement agreement was entered into by the US government and ZTE. Under the terms of the settlement, ZTE agreed to pay a US$8,900 million fine and follow several other rules while the DOC suspended the execution of the restriction and another fine of US$3,000 million.
Mar. 2018	On the 13th, BIS informed ZTE that the suspended sanction would be activated immediately in view of ZTE's violation of the suspension terms laid out in the settlement agreement. On the 23rd, the US government announced an increase in tariffs on a possible US$60 billion worth of imported Chinese goods and restriction on Chinese firms' investment, merger and acquisition activities in US firms.
Apr. 2018	On the 3rd, the Office of the US Trade Representative (USTR) published a proposed list of US$50 billion of Chinese goods subjected to an additional 25% tariffs, covering industries such as aerospace, information and communication technology, robotics, machinery and medicine. On the 16th, the DOC placed a seven-year ban on US firms, restricting them from selling components and parts to ZTE. On the 17th, the US government prohibited its telecoms carriers from spending any federal subsidy on the purchase of any telecoms equipment manufactured by Chinese firms. At the same day, the US started anti-dumping and anti-subsidy investigation on Chinese steel hub products.

(Continued)

(Continued)

Time	Events and progress
May 2018	From the 3rd to the 4th, the first round of trade negotiation between the US and China was held in Beijing, in which China expressed a stern disapproval toward ZTE's being punished beyond what it deserved. On the 13th, Trump tweeted that a fast way was being worked on to get ZTE back into business.
Jun. 2018	On the 7th, a deal was reached to save ZTE from collapse, which included a record fine of US$1 billion in civil penalties and US$400 million in escrow, replacement of the company's board and management personnel within 30 days and the installation of US compliance officers. On the 15th, the US government published the confirmed list of US$50 billion worth of Chinese goods subjected to an additional 25% tariffs.
Jul. 2018	On the 1st, the US government claimed to place extra tariffs on US$500 billion worth of Chinese goods. On the 3rd, the DOC announced an order to partially lift the export restriction on ZTE, valid till 1st August 2018, On the 6th, the US government began to collect an additional 25% tariffs on the first US$34 billion worth of Chinese goods out of the US$50 billion announced. On the 10th, the USTR planned to impose an additional 10% tariffs on US$200 billion of Chinese goods and published another list of goods intended to be levied.
Aug. 2018	On the 1st, the DOC put 44 Chinese companies (8 firms and their 36 subsidiary firms) into its export control list, stopping them from importing US-origin components and technology. On the same day, the US government expressed their inclination to increase the proposed 10% tariffs on the US$200 billion of Chinese goods to 20%.

1.3 Trade War or Hi-tech War

There were only a few precedents in ZTE's case where a large international company was harshly hit by a strong external force.

There were many people who failed to realize or who underestimated what the ZTE incident truly meant or denoted. They thought it was just about a company that breached business regulations, got caught and then severely punished to the brink of shutdown. However, it should be highlighted that the actual situation was that the second largest telecoms company in China was squeezed out by the US, the world's most powerful country, in the beginning of a constantly escalating trade friction during a time of global completion in 5G technology. Was it really that simple as many might think?

To answer that question, we should go back to 18th December 2017. On this day, the US Trump administration published its first National Security Strategy Report, in which China was for the first time in the history of the report named as a strategic competitor that demanded strong and decisive attention. The report also emphasized on the priority to secure the US' economic safety. To understand the significance of the report on setting the trend for America's future strategic position, we should note that apart from being an elaborately-worked-on national security plan which received worldwide attention and gave clear signals to both US allies and rivals, this report had been unconventionally published in the first year of a new administration and issued by the President himself. Herbert McMaster, national affairs assistant to the President, declared that the new National Security Strategy Report provided a major reconsideration of US foreign policies from the last few decades.

It was from the publication of this report that the outside world sensed an obvious change of US strategic attitude towards China. Three months later, no doubt after some good preparation, the Trump administration decided to impose additional tariffs on imported Chinese steel and aluminum products. If we thought that was just another imprudent act of Trump or his typical bargaining strategy, we were wrong. Shortly after that, with the progress of the "301 investigation", Trump accused the Chinese government of practicing forced transfer of technology and signed a memorandum of understanding which intended to put an additional 25% tariffs on US$50 billion of imported Chinese goods.

China's Ministry of Commerce implemented counteraction immediately, placing additional tit-for-tat tariffs on imported American goods worth US$3 billion. Trump responded to China's retaliation with an instruction for the USTR to increase tariffs on more Chinese goods, which was US$500 billion according to his proposal. It was about this time that the US activated the ZTE ban.

In the following three months, China and US negotiators shuttled between Beijing and Washington, D. C. in an intense yet unsuccessful effort to straighten things up. The situation was spiraling downwards, if we might say so, with ZTE and many others struggling with hopelessness.

Many would see by now that the whole saga was far more than simple. What was this "301 investigation" that the Trump administration used as a pretext to wage the trade war on China? The "301 investigation" was a trade investigation carried out under Section 301 in the *Trade Act of 1974* and gave authorization to unilateral actions initiated by the US to deal with those who violated or impaired US interests. It was not the first time that the US applied the "301 clause" to secure its financial interests against China. This was the sixth time actually, and most of the other five took place before China entered the World Trade Organization (WTO).

In the strategic decision to restart the "301 clause" against China, Robert Lighthizer, United States Trade Representative and a China-skeptic, played a leading part. A seasoned attorney and a hawkish top trade adviser to Trump, Lighthizer was nominated and confirmed to serve as Deputy US Trade Representative during the administration of President Ronald Reagan. During that tenure, Lighthizer negotiated over two dozen bilateral international agreements, including a tough one against Japan regarding export restriction on steel products.

By persuading Trump to slap tariffs on everything imported from China in order to win true concession from the Chinese government, Lighthizer wanted to push for substantive changes in China's way of doing business, such as forcing China to end its practice of requiring American companies to open joint ventures with Chinese companies as a condition of doing business there. That would require significant shifts in how China's central government and its manufacturing sector were going to coordinate their activities, which might simply not be possible in the short term.

If we dug a little deeper, we would see there was more things underneath. On 22nd March 2018, when giving his testimony in the US Senate, Lighthizer openly cautioned his colleagues against the impending threat to the US economy imposed by "Made in China 2025", a 10-year national plan to transform China's manufacturing, especially some key industries, to world-leading level by robust investment and technology guarding. The "301 investigation", in which all of the ten industries listed in the 10-year manufacturing blueprint were subject to major US investigation, was the beginning of the efforts aimed to temper China's ambition of dominating the world's most crucial technologies. As Andrew Polk, co-founder of research firm Trivium/China in Beijing, said, "China is trying to achieve a clear goal and America wants to stop it, that's where the competition is."

US Trade Representative, Robert Lighthizer.

The day after the Senate hearing, Trump signed the trade memorandum in which stiff tariffs were placed on US$50 billion worth of Chinese goods from 1,300 categories spanning most of the "Made in China 2025" list.

It was declared in the "301 investigation" report that America needed to alter the institutional factors that were standing in the way of its strategic development and that the tariffs pressure put on China should achieve more than just smoothing out the trade gap, but instead aim at forcing China to change its trade policies and practices to play in a system where American rules dominated. In other words, the Trump administration that was advised by Lighthizer was planning on playing the game of a lifetime, redefining the trade relationship between the world's two largest economies.

The US' deep concern for the "Made in China 2025" program stemmed not only from the possible major shift of economic power it might cause, but also from the uneasiness that China might accelerate to access America's core technology by relevant policies and practices. As a response, China denied forcing technology transfer through regulations and stressed that any policies it implemented were ultimately for maintaining national security and stability.

In fact, if we pause to think about it, it is not possible for a country to become the world's second largest economy and earn its place in manufacturing, technology and innovation merely by forced technology transfer. At the end of the day, it is still the national capacity for innovation that matters most in taking a country far ahead. Besides, instead of a trade war or a technology war which can cause huge losses on both sides, is it not wiser to put all these energy and resources to actually improving something?

To what extent can the US succeed in preventing China from achieving its 2025 ambition? Many international commentaries, including *The Economist*, had a negative answer to that question. The magazine attributed China's remarkable high-tech development to its successful coordination of enterprises, consumers and policies to form a highly efficient development mechanism in which technology, market and management are in balance with and stimulating each other. As long as that mechanism continues to work, China may very well be unstoppable.

1.4 A Report That Tells

At the core of the strategic game between the US and China, whether in the form of a full-blown trade war or a concealed technology war, is the competition for technological hegemony in the semiconductor and telecoms industries. The US is worried that in a future largely defined by semiconductor technologies, China's rise in the telecoms industry, protected by China's industrial policies and left unchecked, would become an unneglectable challenge to the US' semiconductor superiority not only across important economic sectors but also in the US' defense system and military strength.

With such a concern, in March 2017 before Trump's inauguration, the President's Council of Advisers on Science and Technology issued a report titled *Ensuring Long-Term US Leadership in Semiconductors*. To prepare this report, John Holdren, Assistant to the President for Science and Technology and Director of the Office of Science and Technology Policy, set up a working group consisting of industry leaders, eminent researchers and former policymakers. The group included such distinguished names as Paul Otellini, co-chair of the working group and former president and CEO of Intel; Richard Beyer, former chairman and CEO of Freescale Semiconductor; Ajit Manocha, former CEO of Global Foundries; Wes Bush, chairman and CEO of Northrop Grumman; Mike Splinter, former CEO and chairman of Applied Materials; and Paul Jacobs, executive chairman of Qualcomm.

Assistant to the President for Science and Technology, John Holdren.

This report drew a clear picture about the attitude of US elites, think tanks and policymakers towards China's semiconductor industry and, more broadly, China's manufacturing industry. It perceived China's semiconductor industrial policies as a major risk for US semiconductor innovation, competitiveness and integrity. It speculated that China was using industrial policies backed by over US$100 million in government-directed funds to reshape the market, thereby threatening the competitiveness of the US industry. The report thus urged US policies to push back against Chinese industrial policies.

In fact, the US had been the leading light in the semiconductor industry since integrated circuit was born in America and most of the transformative technological innovations started in America as well. Microsoft and Intel dominated the personal computers industry while the Android system from Google and the iOS system from Apple set the rules in the domain of smartphones. At the same time, with China's leading-edge logic device manufacturing capacity and wafer foundry techniques lagging at least one and a half generations behind, as well as its lack of prominent storage device manufacturers, China's performance in the semiconductor field might be near to the US but was far from near enough. So, was it really necessary to use non-market forces to influence Chinese activities as the report imperatively urged?

The report argued that China was aiming to achieve a global leadership position in semiconductor design and manufacturing through non-market means, namely government subsidies and other zero-sum tactics. These activities distorted markets in ways that undermined innovation, subtracted the US market share and put US national security at risk. Even if we put aside the reliability of this argument for a second, it was still noteworthy that the report declared, which was true by the way, that the global semiconductor market was never a completely free market and it had historically been driven in substantial parts by governments and the academia. This statement seemed to justify the ambitious market plans launched by the Chinese government through its policies and tactics, which heralded an aggressive market interfering scheme propelled by the US government.

It was argued in the report that in order to maintain its leadership in the semiconductor industry, US policies should respond to the challenges posed by the industry itself and China by (1) pushing back against Chinese industrial policies; (2) improving the business environment for US-based semiconductor producers; and (3) helping to catalyze transformative semiconductor innovations over the next decade. All of these, the report said, required strong cooperation among government, industry and academia. In the chapter titled *Influencing Chinese Actions*, the report proposed that the US government should revisit its range of tools available, including formal trade agreements, informal trade and investment norms and unilateral tools such as scrutiny of acquisitions by the interagency Committee on Foreign Investment in the United States (CFIUS), to respond to Chinese activities.

In the view of the industry leaders and policymakers who wrote the report, unilateral executive interference on the market by the US government should be encouraged. As a matter of fact, CFIUS voted against a number of Chinese semiconductor companies' applications to acquire US and other country's semiconductor companies, including those of Canyon Bridge towards Lattice, Fujian Grand Chip Investment towards Aixtron from Germany, Chins Resources towards Fairchild Semiconductor, Unisplendour (UNIS) towards Western Digital and Micron Technology, and Hubei Xinyan Investment towards Xcerra. All of these applications were obstructed by the US government; some were blocked before the publication of the report and subsequent blockings would be justified and hailed now that unilateral intervention had been encouraged by the report.

The microchip industry is a tough and multilateral game as companies need to compete for future dominance with new rules to propel the next generation of civilization and development. The report revealed the US' deep concern about China's advantage as a late comer and China's strong momentum of moving forward, as well as the US' own problematic economic structure.

If this 2017 report laid out the strategic principles and plans on securing long-term US leadership in semiconductors, then the newly implemented Electronics Resurgence Initiative (ERI) provided a real example of how the US planned to invest its national strength into influencing semiconductors in its favor.

In June 2018, the 55th ACM/IEEE Design Automation Conference was held in San Francisco, attracting the worldwide participation of IT experts, industry leaders and top university scholars. Officials from the US Defense Advanced Research Projects Agency (DARPA) declared that America was about to launch the ERI, which aimed to bring about the next electronics revolution through a highly-efficient coordination between the national defense industrial base, academia, national laboratories and other innovation hotbeds with an investment of US$2 billion over the next five years.

It was revealed that an investment of US$100 million had already went into the initiative for the R&D of a new set of chips development tool under the collaborative efforts of 15 companies and more than 200 researchers. In fact, a congressional semiconductors caucus aiming at a systematic research of semiconductors industrial policies had kicked into action three years ago. Since then, the US Congressional Research Service and the President's Council of Science and Technology had successively published policy-defining reports in 2016 and 2017.

Why is America so desperate to safeguard its semiconductors industry and so eager to ensure its leadership in the field? When you have gotten used to the economic, political and national security bonuses brought by your front-runner status in electronics and semiconductors, it is impossible to let it slide away. The future-defining technology of 5G and AI, in which semiconductors served as the core and the base, requires state-sponsored transformative innovations. In today's world where Moore's Law is no longer applicable, electronics looking for long-overdue breakthroughs and new science branches emerging at an unprecedented pace, the US is proactively working out its strategic leadership in the next decades, or even the next centuries.

1.5 US-Japan Confrontation in the 1980s

It is not the first time that America is resorting to the practice of unilateral trade protectionism. Back in the 1980s, Japan had already fallen victim to US restriction and sanction. A monthly magazine in Japan called *Choice* published an article in June 2018 titled *US-China Semiconductor War Bound to Flare Up*. The article reviewed the ZTE incident and said that the US launched attacks on individual companies with the excuse of reducing its trade deficits and the threat to prohibit the supply of US-made components. All of these reminded the Japanese of what they once experienced at the hands of the US.

Thirty years ago, the Japanese economy ranked second in the world for gross national production and enjoyed a remarkable trade surplus against the US due to its export-oriented, competitively-priced and good-quality products. Japanese car brands such as Toyota and Honda took up 20% of America's market share at one time. Japanese car exports to America reached US$24 billion, making Japan the biggest car exporter to America. Wilting under Japan's robust market performance, US car manufacturers sacked more than 60,000 employees in the early 1980s. That was just in the car industry. Japan's rise in manufacturing caused many companies in America's Great Lakes area, where the US manufacturing industry was based, to go bust. It also caused large-scale unemployment around the country. The term "Rust Belt" was derived from this period of time and painted a vivid image of what the situation was like back then.

Apart from manufacturing, Japan's semiconductor industry was also in rapid and robust development. Intel, the US chip giant, was plagued with a severe financial crisis because of its inability to compete with Japanese product prices. In 1983, Andrew Grove, the president of Intel and a legend in the semiconductor industry, made a tough yet transformative decision. He decided to give up on storage chips, where Intel lost almost every advantage to Japanese companies, and turned to the development of integrated chips. This bold move saved Intel from collapse and strengthened its leadership for decades to come.

In the year of 1986, the world's top three semiconductor sales volume were from Japanese companies, namely NEC Corporation, Toshiba and Hitachi, and six out of the world's top ten were Japanese companies. Faced with this awkward situation where both money and jobs were lost, the US government turned to trade protectionism and launched unilateral trade investigations and sanctions to crack down on the so-called Japanese economic threat.

During the 1980s, trade friction between the United States and Japan was heating up. Japanese exports were subjected to a total of 24 rounds of US "301 investigation", ranging from textile and steel to technology-based products like automobiles and televisions. While being investigated and on the brink of being sanctioned by the United States, Japan was still relying deeply and widely on the US, not only for military and foreign affairs, but also for its economic development, as determined by Japan's defeat in World War II. Fettered by this severe dependence, Japan could not afford a tit-for-tat reaction against the trade friction initiated by the US. Instead, it took the compromise of setting a limit on its exports to the US and loosening its markets and policies for US companies. This, by the way, is what the US wants to achieve in China currently.

In 1987, the Toshiba incident raised the US-Japan trade tension into its peak and US boycott of Japanese products was at its fiercest. The incident started when Toshiba, the giant Japanese semiconductor company, secretly sold four numerical control tools to the Soviet Union in 1983, which enabled the US rival in the Cold War to develop more advanced submarines. The sale was actually in breach of the regulations of the Paris-based Coordinating Committee for Export to Communist Countries. Four years later, the disclosure of the transaction angered the US government and caused a large-scale condemnation of the Japanese government. Some US congressmen were so enraged that they smashed a Toshiba radio in front of Capitol Hill in Washington, D. C. and demanded that the Japanese company be penalized with a US$15 billion fine and a five-year ban of Toshiba's exports to the United States.

Almost at the same time, the IBM business espionage incident erupted. Employees of Hitachi and Mitsubishi who were involved in stealing IBM technology were arrested by the US government and the two companies were inflicted with severe sanctions. Fujitsu, a Japanese company that was a conspirator in the espionage incident, was forced into a deal with IBM which stipulated it to pay the US company a record-high amount of technology compensation.

The article recalled a series of US attempts to put increasingly excessive pressure on the Japanese export industry. In 1981, Japan was forced

US congressmen smashing a Toshiba radio in front of Capitol Hill in Washington, D. C.

to put a constraint on its automobile exports to the US; in 1983, Japanese motorcycles were levied a 45% tariff by the US government; in 1985, Japan was obliged to increase its import of America agricultural products like beef and oranges; in 1986, the two countries entered into a semiconductor agreement in which Japan had to set a minimum export price for its semiconductor products, promise not to sell cheap to the US and guarantee a certain market share for imported semiconductors; and in 1987, the US put a startling 100% tariff on Japanese televisions and computers. It was plain to see that the US was targeted in its strikes as most of its victims were Japan's most competitive industries. All the more so with the notorious Plaza Accord, which made Japan stand still in the same place for 20 years.

Although the US-Japan trade friction served to force an update of Japan's industrial structure to a certain extent, the negative effect obviously outstripped the positive one. Take Japan's chip industry for example: the number of Japanese companies listed in the world's top 10 semiconductor manufacturers went from 6 in 1986 to 3 in 2005; and in the year 2016, there was only Toshiba struggling to maintain its ranking.

Japan got a bitter and painful idea of what it meant to displease the US, as seen from the IBM business espionage incident and the Toshiba incident. Ever since then, its semiconductor industry entered an Ice Age under the dual impact of a forced self-constraint on its semiconductor exports and an acceptance of at least 20% domestic market share for US products.

The article revealed the secret of America's solution for issues of a large engagement, which was to crack down on individual persons and individual companies and let the small cracks bring the dam down. The US government and industries applied this same effective method to clamp down on China's semiconductor industry. The difference this time, though, is that America is seriously viewing China as an obstacle on its path to maintaining world hegemony. What the US wants is far more than narrowing trade deficits, it has the intention to upend the whole system and policies that supported China's development of semiconductors.

As a matter of fact, trade protectionism has been gaining popularity ever since the 2008 global financial crisis, especially in developed economic entities where anti-globalization sentiment spreads ever so fast. Global trade friction has been speeding up and the year 2015 was the first time in 40 years when international trade growth rate were lower than GDP growth rate.

1.6 A Gray Rhino Crisis

The heated trade dispute between the world's two largest countries casts a light on the Achilles heels of China's semiconductor manufacturing and on America's struggles in maintaining its supremacy in a globalized and depolarized world.

The full-scale export restriction on ZTE by the US DOC involves products ranging from core electronics parts and components, high-end universal chips to foundational software. China's strategic analysts believed that America's aggressiveness is in essence a battle for core technology under the cover of a trade war and a new round of ambitious yet pushy strategic campaign in a new era of science and technology

A "Gray Rhino" is a highly probable, high impact yet neglected threat — Michele Wucker.

revolution. They also noted that America has bared its teeth and revealed itself as a Gray Rhino to be faced with in the future.

Where does America's struggles come from?

The American economy, already devastated by the subprime crisis and affected by its long-time reliance on the finance industry and the outflow of its manufacturing industry, has shifted from a manufacturing-driven one to a service-oriented one.

China, on the other hand, has been consciously improving its manufacturing capacity and techniques in a substantial way and is witnessing the establishment of a multi-layer industrial structure featuring low, medium and high end products.

Against the backdrop of a slowing global economy and constraints in energy and the environment, developed countries are starting to focus on consolidating their own economic core and competing for the commanding heights of future industrial development. The global community has reached a consensus that it is time to create economy stimulus from the supply side albeit it being no easy task. A deep concern about the unknown future is starting to spread around the world.

For many years, China's and America's economies complemented each other well, with China at the low to medium end in the global manufacturing chain and America at the high end. The two were at peace with each other in their respective domain of global distribution. However, China's fast move towards the upper end in recent years has disturbed the monopolistic playground ruled by Western developed countries centered around the US.

Hu Weiwu, CEO of Loongson, explained the scenario in a vivid metaphor of landlord and farmers. When the landlord is happy with collecting taxation and payment and the farmers are satisfied to cultivate in His Lordship's soil, the two sides can basically get along. As farmers save enough to buy their own land to plough on, the landlord is infuriated because he is stripped of both his workforce and his land. There is no stopping the landlord from going all the way to make life difficult for the farmers.

When viewed chronologically, it is easy to see that the trade dispute between China and the US is shifting from low-end industries to high-end industries.

Back in the 1990s, the US government carried out a number of "301 investigations" on Chinese exports. In April 1991, US exerted its special 301 clause [targeted at those countries that are deemed inadequate and ineffective in intellectual property rights (IPR) protection] to investigate China's IPR protection of medicine and chemicals patents, copyrights, and commercial and trademark rights. In the same year, the US put additional punitive tariffs on Chinese textile products, shoes, mechanical equipment and electronic products. In 1994, US initiated another investigation targeted at China's IPR protection in copyrights and trademark rights, and implemented vindictive sanctions on China two years later.

In the 21st century, America enters a new phase of finding fault with China as it starts to focus on China's frontier technology. For example, in 2010, America's "301 investigation" was targeted at China's newly-launched new energy policy. It suspected China of restricting export of important mineral products, providing excessive export subsidy, discriminating against foreign products and companies, and forcing technology transfer.

An American magazine called *Foreign Affairs* published an intriguing article titled *Green Giant: Renewable Energy and Chinese Power* in 2018. The article exclaimed the extent in which China is pushing forward its R&D in green energy technology. Amy Myers Jaffe, the author, likened the 21st century US-China competition in clean energy technology to the US-Soviet space race during the Cold War. Jaffe declared that Chinese breakthrough in the field will become an unneglectable threat to America's ruling status in the global energy market.

Mei Guanqun, a researcher from the Chinese International Economy Exchange Center, explained why there will be trade deficits in the US and why it is impossible for the Trump administration to remove those deficits simply by implementing trade sanctions. Mei noted that America's trade deficits have been there since the US dollar became the international currency after the end of World War II. For the US, it has been there for a good reason. Being the world currency or the number one international reserve currency after the breakdown of the Bretton Woods system, the US dollar is widely and largely demanded by other countries for international settlements and for maintaining their own currencies' value. This entails an outflowing of US dollars into other countries and brings inevitable trade deficits to America. In other words, US trade deficits are natural and inevitable by-products of the US dollar's status as an international currency. It would be impossible to have your cake and eat it; if you choose to enjoy the enormous benefits brought about by being an international currency, you should also bear its consequences, like trade deficits.

Among America's protectionist moves in recent years, the competition for control over telecoms security involving chips is particularly intensified. It is essentially a competition for a stronger position in maintaining national security and safeguarding future economic growth.

On one hand, our world is experiencing an unprecedented digital globalization process in which data resources, especially big data, are transforming the way our world used to operate and the competition for dominance over strategic data resources has never been fiercer. According to a strategic analyst in the Chinese Science and Technology

Department, about 50% of the world's trade in services is carried out digitally and 12% of the trade in commodities is made through the global e-commerce network.

On the other hand, many countries have been rolling out plans and programs to revive the manufacturing industry and to develop artificial intelligence. Boosting economy and updating industry structure have become the targets of many governments. The national plans that the US has put into effect to restore its manufacturing industry include the Manufacturing Promotion Act, Advanced Manufacturing Partnership, Strategy for American Leadership in Advanced Manufacturing, National Network for Manufacturing Innovation (now called Manufacturing USA). It has also offered strong sponsorship for 15 Institutions of Manufacturing Innovation (IMI). For the development of intelligent manufacturing, Germany has put forward its Manufacturing 4.0 Plan and General Electric (GE) is promoting the idea of Manufacture Internet. China's Made in China 2025 program is similarly a vision for the transformation and upgrading of Chinese manufacturing. It aims to purposefully guide investment flow and technology innovation rather than just implement compulsory regulations.

Against this background, the United States has put up a stricter and sterner censorship against Chinese companies who have applied or are going to apply for acquisition of US tech companies. In September 2017, an ongoing acquisition of a US chips manufacturer called Lattice by a private equity was voted down by the Trump administration because the equity was found to be supported also by Chinese capital. This case apparently sent a clear message that in order to prevent China's penetration into sensitive industries associated with US national security and core technology, the US government was prepared to crank up the power of its censorship on foreign involvement in these areas. On 28th January, Ant Financial, a leading internet finance company in China under the Alibaba Group, was forced to cease its acquisition negotiation with Moneygram, an US fast remittance company founded in 1940, because the US Supervision Department did not approve of it. In the same year on 12th March, Trump signed an executive order to suspend the acquisition of Qualcomm by Broadcom on national security grounds. The effectiveness of this kind of censorship had been recognized and even implicitly encouraged in many US government reports. Apart from resorting to censorship, the US also worked with its allies to influence global exports in order to beef up its domestic investment environment.

The PRISM program (in which the US National Security Agency collected internet communications from various US internet companies) revealed a cruel fact that a nation's telecoms security could be under permanent threat and surveillance if its core telecoms technology could not achieve self-sustainability and need to rely on another country's design and deployment. The hackings into Ukraine's national power grid and Iran's nuclear power station were grave reminders of this fact. These incidents also demonstrated that a country's national security would be threatened by the absence of core strategic technology. The Trump administration made it clear that the US government adopted a broader realm of protectionism in economy, industry and national security, rather than trade alone. This was reflected in the latest round of "301 investigation" focused on China's IPR protection and technology transfer in high-tech fields including telecoms, integrated circuits, semiconductors and new energy automobiles. In the foreseeable future, this kind of US maneuvers against China would likely not stop for good.

Edward Snowden, the whistleblower of the PRISM program.

This current round of trade friction and sanction against China initiated by the Trump administration is not on the spur of a moment nor a conventional bargaining chip. The two countries are in a race to speed up transformative innovations in core technologies, which could in the end determine the future of the two largest economic entities in the world.

From the perspective of America and its policies, it seems the global leader is bent on sticking to the old global order in this fast-changing world. Quite a few American elites believed that the benefits brought by globalization could not balance the negative impacts it is causing to the US and it is time for fundamental changes. America's regress to anti-globalization and protectionism is not so much about slogans and stances but more about self-interests.

The ZTE incident and the consequent long-lasting trade friction are just the beginning of the relentless pressure the US is going to inflict on China for a very long time to come.

It was revealed that the Trump administration was setting out to establish an independent institution with similar functions as the CFIUS which worked on a trans-department basis. The plan was faced with disagreement inside the US government. However, according to a Trump staff who had the knowledge, the China hawks had won the rhetoric salvos and the White House had informed related departments to designate representatives to the Treasury Department to work on the mechanism of this new establishment.

This move sparked a widespread concern that Chinese investment in America could further slack off. Statistics from Rhodium Group showed a 90% year-on-year drop in Chinese direct investment in the US during the first half of 2018, plunging to US$1.8 billion, as contrasted with US$46 billion in the year 2016.

The trade dispute between China and the US is undoubtedly moving towards high-tech industries. As a matter of fact, global competition involving new technologies and new industries will only get fiercer and international trade friction targeted at frontier industries is only a part of that competition.

Many economists and politicians around the world asserted that waging a trade war in this era is an obsolete, backward and ineffective way of dealing with problems. No one could know what this clash between the world's two largest countries would lead to.

Optimists opined that while the two parties are engaged in conflicts and collisions, they also have to sit at the table to talk to each other, hence this whole series of happenings would possibly evolve along the plot of disputes, hard bargains, more disputes, harder bargains and finally compromises and conditions. They believed that the conflicts and collisions are bold stakes by the two countries to drive a good bargain at the table.

Pessimists, on the other hand, reminded us that the trade friction between China and the US is going to be chronically grim, especially when the two economic powers are increasingly engaged in a state of push and pull. They warned the optimists of a dangerous possibility that the US-China trade war could go all the way if no compromise is to be obtained. They are concerned that if such a situation arises, it could expand into a full-blown rivalry across finance, resources and security, the US could put a full-scale lid on China by drawing on its hegemony status established after World War II which spans across trade, finance and military, and the recovery of the world's economy could be completely reversed.

It is a great uncertainty that our human race is heading into.

References

1. Donald J. Trump, Tony Schwartz Trump. *The Art of the Deal* [M]. Random House US. 2004.
2. John P. Holdren. *Report to The President: Ensuring Long-Term US Leadership in Semiconductors* [R]. 2017.
3. Wei Da. *The Real Intention behind the US Trade War on China* [N]. Union Morning Paper. 2018–04.
4. *US-China Semiconductors War Bound to Flare up* [J]. Choice. 2018–06.
5. *Green Giant: Renewable Energy and Chinese Power* [N]. Foreign Affairs. 2018–06.
6. Mi Zhou & Yin Sheng. *The Development of ZTE* [M]. Contemporary China Publishing House. 2005.

Chapter 2

Microchips in the Global Power Game

Overture

In the global power game, check and countercheck is critical in capturing the leadership role in core technology, and microchips dominance has become the unquestionable lethal weapon.

The Chinese are worried that Washington's penchant for China bashing would be taken to an entirely new level.

Meanwhile, dependency on others for core technology must be stopped if China intends to fend off the heavy attack from the US.

In the face of an unrelenting series of bans, China's microchips industry is once again going through a collective anxiety. Countless people are pondering the next step in China's semiconductor development.

This is the winter of disappointment, and this is the spring of hope. For a tree to grow upwards to a higher and brighter place, its roots need to grow downwards to the depth and darkness of the earth.

> **What does not kill me, makes me stronger.**
> **— Friedrich Wilhelm Nietzsche**

2.1 Will the Chinese IT Industry be Paralyzed?

The bleak outlook of ZTE induced by the US export restriction reminded us of a classic case of failure in risk management, that is,

Ericsson being forced out of the mobile phone market by a sudden incident. Ericsson's tragedy began when a Philips chips production factory in New Mexico, US broke out in fire in March 2000. After the fire, the factory was unable to produce the microchips Ericsson needed for at least half a year, which resulted in a forced stop of Ericsson's phone production and an ultimate fade-out of Ericsson's share in the global phone market.

Compared with Ericsson 20 years ago, the trouble ahead of ZTE is far more complicated and severe because this is a time of rising US-China trade friction and the shift of the "301 investigation" to a much bigger goal. The Chinese IT industry will be going into a bleak winter.

1. *A Serious Heart Ailment*

The developed countries' long-time restraint on China's integrated circuit industry has to a large extent handicapped China's capacity to develop high-end microchips and software reliable enough to be put into large-scale application. The result is that most of China's computer systems and billions of its smartphones are working with imported microchips, running without a Chinese heart. Besides this heart ailment, China also faces security uncertainties.

It is not just ZTE who is in danger. If the US toughens up its actions, will the entire Chinese IT industry be reduced to a paralysis?

This is a very disturbing yet realistic question. ZTE to a certain extent epitomizes the Chinese IT industry, its origin and its outlook. While a huge number of high-tech products have been produced in the world's factory that is China and sold around the world with a "Made in China" label, most Chinese IT companies still depend on foreign technology and imported components, especially microchip-related ones. Imported microchips are used widely in IT applications in China, like telecoms, internet, medical equipment, high-end manufacturing, traffic control, even water and electricity supplies.

It is true in a way that China's status of being the world's factory can never happen if not for the foreign heart. According to statistics from the US, of all the exports from China to the US, smartphones and computers take up 13.8% and 9.8% respectively. They take up the largest two portions of the total export value amounting to US$120 billion and contribute the most to China's trade surplus with the US.

If we add up the number of smartphones and computers that China has exported to the whole world, it is even more astonishing. Eighty percent of the world's smartphones and 95% of the world's computers are made in China.

However, "Made in China" may not be the true story, "Assembled in China" is a more apt label. The large number of smartphones and computers exported from China, among many other products, are assembled by the world's factory through original equipment manufacturers (OEMs) as represented by Foxconn. Most of the core components in the assembly line like microchips, display panels and electronic parts are imported from developed countries.

Foxconn, the world's largest OEM company, is founded in Taiwan and goes on to prosper in mainland China. Its developmental history is a testament to the remarkable journey of the Chinese IT industry from a blank page to an influential force in a space of 30 years. Foxconn is also an active participant in China's industry transformation and restructuring.

Foxconn is originally a small factory, established in 1974, which makes plastic knobs for black and white televisions. Its founder Guo Taiming has probably never thought that his factory would one day made 40% of the world's electronic products and be the first in human history whose employees are in the millions.

The now impressive manufacturing base of Foxconn in Longhua, Shenzhen started out as a small factory with no more than hundreds of workers back in 1988. It is this factory that is responsibe for assembling more than half of the 2 billion iPhones sold to the world since 2007. We call Steve Jobs the founding father of the legendary Apple brand, and we may well call Guo Taiming the titan amongst the producers of Apple products.

CEO of Foxconn, Guo Taiming.

However, Foxconn is actually living at the lowest end of the industrial chain with a rather slim profit. For every Apple tablet sold at US$499, its assembler Foxconn only gets US$11.20 in return.

OEMs, in other words, is the lowest-end labor force working for big international companies. They make products according to upstream companies' design and technology, and then sell them in their names. With pivotal parts of the industrial chain being dominated and controlled by upstream big players, OEMs are left to seek profit from the differences in labor costs. Foxconn has surely tasted every bit of the bitterness as an OEM.

Ever since the implementation of China's reform and opening-up policy, labor-intensive and export-oriented OEM factories have continued to play an important role in providing domestic employment and expanding exports. They have made remarkable contributions to China's fast economic growth, but this mode of development that relies heavily on low-cost labor instead of core technologies has made it hard for China's economy to transform and update.

Enormous output volumes but meager margins depict the dilemma faced by many Chinese OEM factories at the threshold of sweeping industrial transformations. These companies' gross earnings are on a continuous slide despite their efforts to further cut down on labor costs. An enterprise which pins its operational performance on overloading its employees is actually dulling its vivacity and competitiveness, and it is unhelpful to the mission of achieving sustainability.

Therefore, Foxconn could not be satisfied with the label of the King of Outsourcing and it has been taking restructuring actions to shake it off. Among its actions include acquisition of Nokia's smartphone business, merger with display panels manufacturer Sharp, investments in Chinese ride-hailing app DiDi and other self-driving automobile companies, and the recent ambitious yet frustrated attempt to acquire Toshiba's microchips business. Developing its self-owned brands is also a crucial part of Foxconn's transformation strategy.

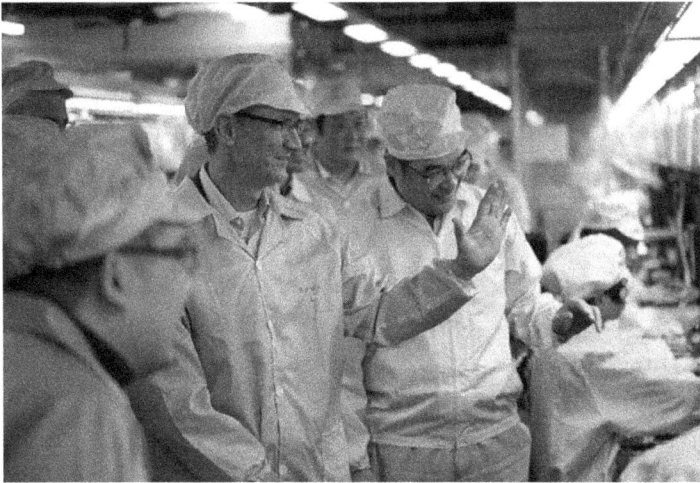

Apple's CEO Tim Cook visiting Foxconn's iPhone production line in Zhengzhou Technology Park.

Just before the launch of Foxconn Industrial Internet IPO in China's A-share market at the start of 2018, Guo declared at the company's shareholders meeting that Foxconn is no longer just an outsourcing factory and it is on course to transform into a technology-oriented enterprise. The King of Outsourcing is seeking higher places in the global industrial chain.

The word interdependency might best describe the characteristic of our modern, industrialized and information society. From raw materials to product development to manufacturing and marketing, the whole industrial chain depends on division and collaboration of work among various companies scattered from downstream to upstream sectors. Such an interdependent relationship might continue to be mutually beneficial in an idealized and stabilized global market. After all, the irreversible trend of globalization has made international cooperation across sectors, especially in high-tech industries, a necessity. Furthermore, the current global industrial chain has formed a division system in which countries can fit into their own roles and their performances are increasingly interconnected with one another. However, the relationship might stumble in the actual operation and development of the global market, where downstream participants aspire to move towards high value-added divisions that have already been occupied and controlled by upstream participants. These companies, as a response, would take every measure to prevent the newcomers from climbing up to compete for bigger slices of the cake. The newcomers, as a result, would get stuck in a very difficult situation because they do not have their own core technologies, equipment and market share.

As long as the global market continues to be dominated by the rule-setters, those companies in the downstream would not have a say on where and how they want to march into their future and they need to be prepared for a long-term fight.

2. *A Startling Gap*

On the night of 18th April 2018, several days after ZTE was slapped with the export ban by the US government, a special forum was held in Zhongguancun in Beijing, dubbed China's Silicon Valley, to discuss this incident. A huge concern shared by most of the attendants was the future of China's hi-tech industry in the face of America's relentless attack.

At the forum, a set of alarming statistics from a report on China's IT industry performance indicated a close-to-zero market share of China's self-made microchips in products such as computer systems, general electronic equipment, telecoms devices, storage devices, display and video systems. Although the shocking number may have exaggerated the underperformance of China's manufacturing capacity of microchips, it is still a widely accepted reality that China's microchips industry lags behind world-leading techniques in many aspects.

If we look at China's performance in the four industrial domains of the microchips manufacturing chain, namely microchips design, wafer foundry, package and testing, and equipment and raw materials, we will see China's deficiencies more clearly. For example, in the fields of wafer foundry and packaging and testing where no demanding technical barriers exist, Chinese companies can be expected to catch up with world-class techniques within three to five years, albeit doing it in a right way. However, when it comes to chips design where pervasive technical barriers and protection make innovation ever so hard for other countries, China may need much more time and effort to catch up with those world-leading companies.

Inside Knowledge

Integrated Circuit Design

An integrated circuit (also referred to as a microchip) is a set of electronic circuits on one small flat piece of semiconductor material that is normally silicon. To arrange so many circuits onto a tiny piece of silicon, engineers need to design their layouts like how an architect designs building projects. The first step of the whole designing process is setting up system specification, which includes feasibility study, die size estimate and function analyses. It is almost similar to deciding on the structure of a building, the size of each room, the rules and regulations to follow and the functions expected of the building.

The second step of circuit design is when designers implement the functional models agreed during the first step into a hardware description language. In other words, the design drawing in this step comes in the form of coding languages. Finalization of the drawing also involves repeated review and revision in order to reduce the number of functionality bugs.

Coming up next is the physical design stage in which the coding design in the second step is mapped into actual geometric representations of all electronic devices that will go on the chip. There is a list of computer-aided design software to help designers with this process. For example, electronic design automation (EDA) software like Cadence[1] can easily facilitate the transformation of complicated coding language into visualized physical design in the form of printed circuit board (PCB). With the actualization of the PCB, an integrated circuit is thus successfully designed.

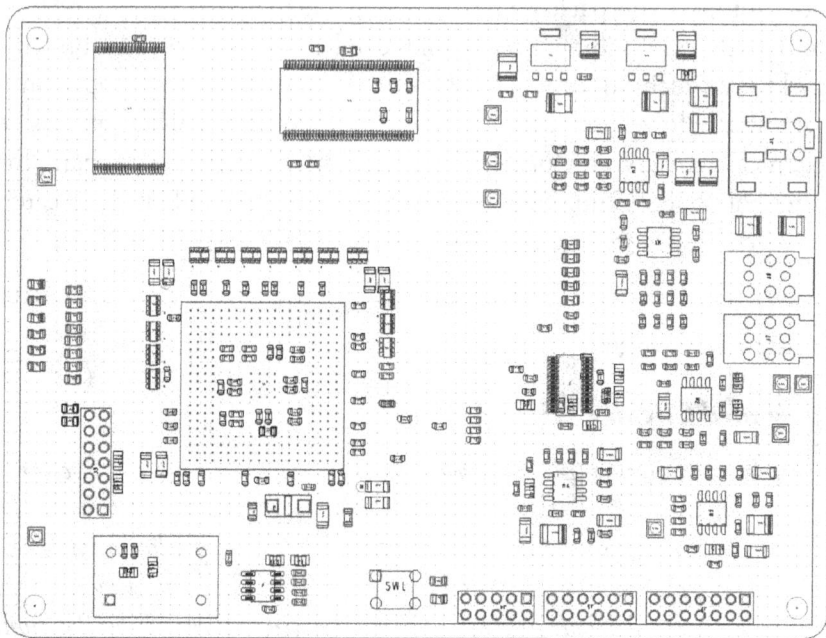

A PCB designed with the help of Cadence.

---

[1] Cadence Design Systems, Inc. is a California-based American company specializing in EDA technologies and electronic engineering service. It is the world's largest supplier of integrated circuit designing tools.

This diagram shows the proportion of China-origin integrated circuits used in the Chinese IT industry.

Fields	Equipment	Core integrated circuit used	Proportion of China-origin microchips used
Computer systems	Server	MPU	0
	Personal computer	MPU	0
	Industrial-used computer	MCU	2%
General electronic devices	Programmable logic device	FPGA/EPLD	0
	Digital signal processing equipment	DSP	0
Communication devices	Mobile communication terminal	Application Processor	18%
		Communication Processor	22%
		Embedded MPU	0
		Embedded DSP	0
	Core network device	NPU	15%
Storage devices	Semiconductors storage	DRAM	0
		NAND FLASH	0
		NOR FLASH	5%
		Image Processor	5%
Display and video systems	High-definition television (HDTV)/ smart TV	Display Processor	5%
		Display Driver	0

After going through the design process, we may begin to understand why designing is the most challenging industrial domain in the microchips manufacturing chain. Although China's leading integrated circuit producers like Hisilicon and Spreadtrum have made statisfying progress in developing processor chips for application in mobile terminals, China's semiconductor companies still rely heavily on foreign companies to provide IP and designing tools for chips used in personal computers and servers. For example, 95% of the smartphones and tablet personal computers used around the world are based on the semiconductor

IP provided by ARM, a global semiconductor and software design company, and the EDA software market is dominated by three American companies, namely Synopsys, Cadence and Mentor. This severe dependence on foreign technologies have confined most of the mainland Chinese integrated circuit designing companies to the development of application chips for specific and narrow uses only, according to China Center for Information Industry Development.

When it comes to wafer foundry, it would take Chinese mainland companies who are two to three generations behind the world's most advanced manufacturing techniques at least five years to catch up. Take Semiconductor Manufacturing International Corporation (SMIC), China's largest domestic semiconductor OEM factory, for example. For a very long time, SMIC's highest-level manufacturing technique had been stuck at 28 nanometer and it was not until August 2018 did the company successfully develope the technique for 14 nanometer microchips. Taiwan Semiconductor Manufacturing Company (TSMC), on the other hand, was able to produce 28 nanometer microchips as early as 2011 and has been devoting itself to the development of 7 nanometer technique since then. TSMC is responsible for producing most of Qualcomm, Broadcom and NVIDIA's microchips. Even mainland China's self-designed commercial-used chips, like Huawei's Kirin series developed by Hisilicon, have been outsourced to the Taiwan-based company.

Statistics from the China Semiconductors Industry Association showed that out of the 1,380 integrated circuit designing companies in mainland China, nearly all are small ones with weak R&D capacity, and none is among the world's top 20 semiconductor manufacturers.

Inside Knowledge

Nanometer technique in microchips manufacturing

In many awe-inspiring news about microchips development, we can often hear specifications like 22 nanometer, 14 nanometer or 7 nanometer, but what do they mean really? And, is a smaller number synonymous with better technique?

To get the questions answered, we need to first get an idea about how minute nanometer actually is. Many may know that one nanometer is one millionth of a millimeter, but to put it in a clear and visual way, we can imagine it to be the length of ten thousandth of one hair's diameter. That is how tiny it is.

After understanding how minuscule nanometer is, it is now important to know the significance of scaling down the size of transistors built into microchips. First, smaller transistors allow for more of them to be laid on semiconductor chips of similar size, which translates to more exquisite designs for the increasingly complicated functions required of integrated circuits. Second, smaller transistors can enhance the operation efficiency of processors by accelerating the current transport rate which, at the same time, works to lower power consumption. Lastly, smaller sizes are more compatible with today's lightweight mobile devices.

Despite all the benefits brought by smaller-sized microchip components, it is impossible presently to minimize transistors as much as we want because of the confinement of current physical rules. If microchips go any smaller into a world counted in single-digit nanometer, like the size of atoms and atomic nucleus (the diameter of an atom is around 0.1 nanometer), then physics would enter a brand-new sphere where a yet fully unraveled theory called quantum mechanics would come into play and the physical rules applicable in our macro world would be totally upended. Therefore, if scientists and engineers wish to further minimize the size of microchips in the world of nanometers, they will need to first make a breakthrough in physics.

From core parts and components to production equipment then to designing and manufacturing, the microchips industrial chain encompasses a series of interconnected links. China may need to address the following four obvious weak links.

(1) Heavy reliance on foreign semiconductor technology

Although China has developed its own microchips to use in the field of national defense and security, the majority of its civil-application microchips still rely on technology and core components imported from world-leading companies. Among these companies, American ones with their defining and exclusive technologies exert an absolute domination on the global semiconductor industry. What China is desperately lacking in the industry is the technological advantage accumulated by Western countries in the last decades by having a head start.

(2) Heavy reliance on foreign suppliers for advanced semiconductor manufacturing equipment

Advanced Semiconductor Materials Lithography (ASML), the world's largest semiconductor equipment manufacturer, designs and produces the most accurate and efficient lithography machine in the industry. It supplies to leading chip producers all over the world, preferentially to Samsung, TSMC and Intel because these three constitute the main shareholders of the Netherlands-based company. ASML's lithography machine's annual output is no more than a dozen and its price easily reaches as high as US$100 million. In order to add one lithography machine produced by ASML into their production line, Chinese companies need to first wait in the queue to put an order, then wait for another two years for the delivery of the machine and finally spend

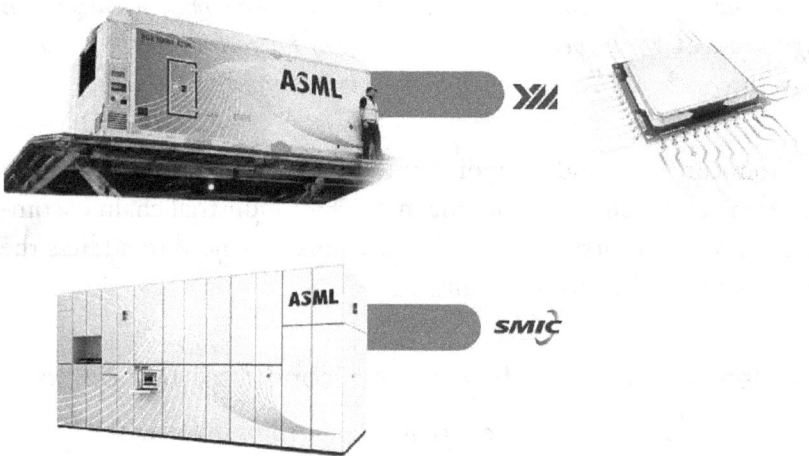

The two lithography machines Chinese companies bought from ASML, at a cost of around 1.23 billion yuan.

about one year on the production line testing. Three years of waiting plus a lot of money will land you the world's most advanced lithography machine, but three years of waiting also pull you further apart from the front runners.

(3) Severe constraint from upstream hidden champion companies

There are certain small-to-medium companies in the global industrial chain who, though not very famous, dominate the market share in a specific field. We call them the hidden champions. Synopsys and Cadence, two American companies, are such hidden champions who dominate the global EDA software market for integrated circuit designing. For a while after the US government put the export restriction on ZTE, Cadence stopped its supply to the Chinese company, which caused even more chaos for the battered telecoms company.

The hidden champions in the domain of high-end electronic material manufacturing and supplying, like silicon wafer, photomask, photoresist, ceramic plate and bonding wire, are also outside China. If any of these companies reduces its supply to China or just stop supplying at all, China's semiconductor industrial chain could face a large-scale shutdown.

(4) No trump card for equivalent deterrence

The complex and interdependent nature of the semiconductor industrial chain determines that there would be no country which can place all relevant manufacturing domains under its control. As pointed out by Wang Huan, the Director of the International Cooperation Department of China Electronics Association, international specialization has been and will be fundamental in the development of the global semiconductor industry. In many cases, he said, the world's leading companies are in patent cross-license agreements with one another, which make sure that they each possess certain trump cards and poses equivalent deterrence to one another. Presently, in China, there are none of such semiconductor companies who has either a dominating technology or a trump card.

2.2 China's Dependency on Western Semiconductors

Can you imagine what the world will be like if microchips exist no more? Computers cannot be operated, the internet cannot be connected, radars go blind, telecommunications shut down, automated mechanized equipment become useless lumps of steel... It is not just science fiction, but a potential reality in an information war, a modern type of war pivoted on semiconductors and microchips. After the ZTE incident, Zhang Shaozhong, who is a widely respected military expert in China, spoke out on the internet. He asked, "Why China did not start earlier to develop its own semiconductor industry if microchips are so strategically important? Are things really what we think they are?"

Whenever China starts to set its mind on developing semiconductors, Zhang continued to explain, it is told by the US that they have got it all under control and China does not need to bother, and that specialization in the global industrial chain is the future trend and a win-win way to go.

It is true that in high-tech industries like telecommunications and intelligent manufacturing, a globalized industrial structure and supply chain have been well in place and they have brought out the comparative advantage of each country's specialization. Take microchips used in smartphones for example. In the well-developed and mature global supply chain for the manufacturing of the dozens of chips built into one smartphone, certain companies are specialized in semiconductor development and certain companies are focused on circuit integration. On the big stage of semiconductor development, no one country, not even the US, can act the whole play all on its own.

In that sense, not only ZTE but also other globally recognized high-tech companies like Apple, could face a supply chain crisis in the face of a stifling export restriction.

1. *China Has No Core Technologies?*

In the beginning of the 1990s when America's newly-won Gulf War was hailed by the US media as a modernized information war in which silicon triumphed over steel, Akio Morita and Shintaro Ishihara declared in their best-selling book *The Japan That Can Say No: Why Japan Will*

Be First Among Equals that the US could not have won the war but for Japanese semiconductor chips.

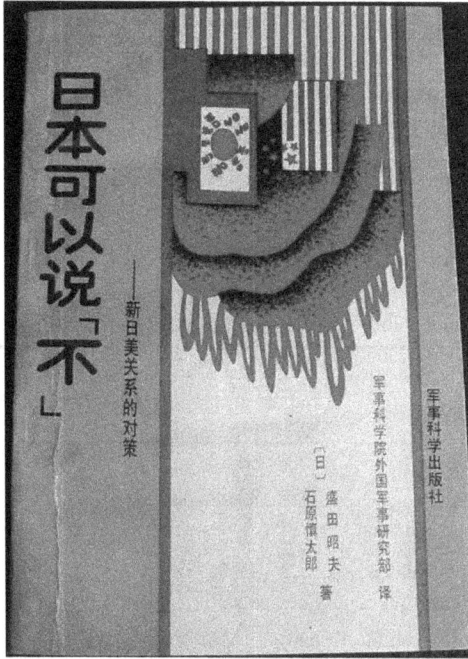

The Japan That Can Say No: Why Japan Will Be First Among Equals, coauthored by Akio Morita and Shintaro Ishihara.

From the authors' perspective, Japan's high-tech industry at that time was five years ahead of America's and any export restriction of core components from Japan's side would have driven America to the end of its wits. If Japan was given another chance, the authors of the book contended, it should have said no to America.

If a country as dominating on the world stage as America was relying on a large amount of electronic component imports, China could possibly be even more dependent on foreign semiconductor companies. However, China is essentially different and so are Chinese companies. No matter how bad the fight is between the US and its semiconductor suppliers/strategic followers such as Japan, Korea and Europe, the latter three would never dare to seize the US by the throat.

When ZTE was seized by the throat by the US, there was a tide of voices criticizing the company of not investing enough into research and development of core technologies. But is it fair to accuse China's second largest semiconductor company of slacking off on R&D efforts?

Firstly, let us look at the statistics published by the World Intellectual Property Organization (WIPO) in 2017 on the ranking of international patent applications via the PCT. The numbers showed ZTE at second place with 2,965 international patent applications, followed by Intel, Mitsubishi, Qualcomm, LG, Samsung and Sony. It was the 8th year in a row that ZTE made it to the top three list.

International patent applications ranking published by WIPO.

PCT tracking	Change in PCT ranking	Applicant	Place of incorporation	2016	2017
1	1	Huawei Technologies Co., Ltd.	China	3692	4024
2	–1	Zhongxing Telecommunication Equipment Corporation	China	4123	2965
3	4	Intel Corporation	US	1692	2637
4	0	Mitsubishi Electric Corporation	Japan	2053	2521
5	–2	Qualcomm Incorported	US	2466	2163
6	–1	LG Electronics Inc.	S. Korea	1888	1945
7	1	BOE Technology Group Co., Ltd.	China	1673	1818
8	1	Samsung Electronics Co., Ltd.	S. Korea	1672	1757
9	1	Sony Corporation	Japan	1665	1735
10	1	Telefonaktiebolaget LM Ericsson (Publ)	Sweden	1608	1564
11	1	Microsoft Technology Licensing, LLC	US	1528	1536
12	–6	Hewlett-Packard Development Company, L.P.	US	1742	1519
13	2257	LETV Holding (Beijing) Co., Ltd.	China	9	1397
14	–1	Robert Bosch Corpartion	Germany	1274	1354
15	0	Panasonic Intellectual Property Management Co., Ltd.	Japan	1175	1280
16	2	Koninklijke Philips Electronics N.V.	Netherland	1137	1077
17	0	Siemens Aktiengesellschaft	Germany	1138	1063
18	–2	Shenzhen China Star Optoelectronics Technology Co., Ltd.	China	1163	972
19	–4	Fujifilm Corporation	Japan	968	970
20	–3	Denso Corporation	Japan	986	968

PCT tracking	Change in PCT ranking	Applicant	Place of incorporation	2016	2017
21	−7	Sharp Corporation	Japan	1205	963
22	−2	Olympus Corporation	Japan	1077	934
23	−1	Hitachi Corporation	Japan	1047	923
24	−3	NEC Corportaoin	Japan	1056	899
25	1	LG Chem, Ltd	S. Korea	671	850
26	−7	Halliburton Energy Services, Inc	US	1097	798
27	3	Google Inc.	US	584	789
28	4	Alibaba Group	China	452	707
29	−4	Murata Manufacturing Co., Ltd	Japan	681	684
30	−3	3m Innovative Properties Company	US	653	678
31	−3	Procter & Gamble Company	US	624	566
32	77	Tencent Compurer Systems Co, Ltd	China	172	560
33	−4	Basf Se	Germany	598	556
34	45	Yulong Computer Telecommumication Scientific (Shenzhen) Co., Ltd	China	256	517
35	4	Hitachi Automotive Systems, Ltd	Japan	396	503
36	−2	Konica Minolta, Inc	Japan	449	492
37	1	Schaeffler Technologies AG & Co. KG	Germany	406	489
38	8	Sabic Global Technologies B.V.	Netherland	359	488
39	−4	University of California	US	434	482
40	240	Guangdong Oppo Mobile Telecommunications Co., Ltd	China	80	474
41	15	Autonetworks Technologies, Ltd	Japan	320	452
42	−5	DOW Global Technologies Inc.	US	415	421
43	−3	Bayerische Motoren Werke Aktiengesellechaft	Germany	383	414
44	6	Compagnie Generale Des Etablissements Michelin	France	343	411
45	−1	General Electric Company	US	364	407
46	11	NTN Corporation	Japan	318	398
47	−11	Kyocera Corporation	Japan	427	377
48	3	Applied Materials, Inc.	US	336	359
49	15	Beijing Xiaomi Technology Co., Ltd	China	298	354
50	−9	Corning Incorporated	US	379	520

Hou Weigui, the founder of ZTE and one of the leading technical experts in the field, knew fully well the role of R&D in an IT company. He spared no effort in developing new technologies during his 30 years of top office in the company.

There is a popular saying among Chinese high-tech companies that third-raters profit on labor, second-raters profit on products, first-raters profit on technology and the most capable of all profit on patents. Hou aspired to bring his company into the rank of the most capable enterprises such as Qualcomm which earned its profits on intellectual property. To achieve that, he set up three research institutions in America in 1998 to develop new generations of telecoms networking technologies. By 1999, the company had mastered the technology needed for developing application-layer software, radio frequency circuit, baseband circuit and some core microchips integration.

In 2002, when ZTE's mobile phone business was first set up in Shanghai, Hou flew to the R&D centers every month to boost the morale of the staff working very hard in the centers. ZTE could have chosen to be an OEM, like numerous other mainland China and Taiwan companies, but it was determined to blaze its own trail in the mobile phone sector, just like what Nokia did. Although many people thought the path of independent development could turn out to be a majorly wrong one, Hou was devoted to it all the time.

The company also put much effort into microchips development. Although the results were not satisfactory enough to cover all of its own demand for chips, the sales volume of its self-developed integrated circuit reached 7.6 billion yuan in 2017.

It is fair to say that ZTE has invested whatever resources it has to develop its own core technologies, but it is just not enough in the face of a strong opponent and a severe pressure. The same could be said of the entire Chinese microchips industry — it has tried and is still trying, but the water is too deep and the road too long.

We have elaborated on the weakness of China's semiconductor industry, but at the same time we need to highlight a fact — China is one of the few countries in the world that has formed an integrated industrial chain with competitiveness in each sector. Statistics showed that the global market share of China's self-developed microchips in 2017 stood at 7.78%, somewhat diminutive compared to China's annual microchips consumption volume, but it was equal to Germany and lagging behind only America, Korea and Japan.

China is also well aware of its moderate performance in semiconductors, especially when contrasted against America's overwhelming superiority. In 2017, China was the world's largest market for integrated circuit for four years consecutively. Most of the circuits, ironically, had to be imported.

Numbers showed that in 2017, China imported 377 billion pieces of microchips with a value totaling US$260 billion, whereas its imported crude oil in the same year amounted to a total value of US$162 billion. China is almost completely reliant on imports for state-of-the-art microchips used in computer processors, automobile controlling systems and intelligent networking systems.

In an industry that is commonly characterized as high value-added, China's IT companies can only be contented with a return rate of about 2–3% because of a severe lack of core technologies. Many in the Chinese industry would joke that money made from exporting a computer is only enough to buy vegetables. On the other hand, foreign companies whom China imports microchips from, make more than US$10 million every year just by selling microprocessor chips to China.

The ZTE incident has indeed sounded the alarm bell for every participant in the global division system, who may be competitive in a certain aspect but can be easily taken apart by external pressure.

Lack of core technologies not only puts China's economy into the hands of others but also endangers China's overall information security and even national security. The Microsoft 'black screen' incident and the HNC (Huazhong Numerical Control) sanction incident were both harsh lessons related to the lack of core technologies. Li Guojie, an academician from the Chinese Academy of Engineering (CAE) and the honorary president of China Computer Association, said that China has no other choice or shortcut but to develop its own technological deterrence strength.

2. *The Challenges Ahead*

Did China invest in the development and deployment of the semiconductor industry earlier on? Yes, it did. The strategic value of microchips to a country is always recognized by China.

ZTE, Huawei and many other computer and electronics producers in China have been putting money and talents into semiconductor development. However, why did this rapidly evolving hi-tech industry not produce any core technologies of adequate competitiveness and deterrence? What is behind the development bottleneck in China's semiconductor industry?

Our last three chapters will try to answer these questions by revealing the uneasy turn of events in China's semiconductor development and exploring some strategic propositions China is faced with. Before that, we will briefly summarize the three long-standing challenges which long existed and will continue to exist in China's semiconductor industry.

(1) Importance of investment

Wang Huan, a researcher from China's Institute of Electronics, reminded us that the microchips industry is a typically investment-driven one. It is almost impossible to achieve any remarkable progress in semiconductors if technology and market share have not been accumulated step by step and year by year through repeated investment of money and people. However, the reality in China is that not every company has the money and the people, and those who have them do not have enough time to climb to the mountain top step by step.

The below table shows the ranking of R&D investment of world-leading semiconductor companies like Intel, Samsung and TSMC in 2016. The total investment of the top three in the table, Intel, Qualcomm and Broadcom, exceeded China's total investment of 138 billion yuan (about US$20 billon) in 2016. Let us zoom in to look at individual Chinese company's R&D investment in 2016. For example, Hisilicon, mainland China's largest microchips designing company, invested US$1 billion which is equivalent to 1/12 of Intel's investment; SMIC, mainland China's largest microchips manufacturer, invested a mere US$318 million. There was an even bigger gap between Chinese companies and global industrial leaders.

Ranking of R&D investment by worldleading semiconductor companies in 2016.

Name	R&D investment (US$ billion)	Ranking	Year-on-year increase	Sales volume (US$ billion)	Ranking	Year-on-year increase	Investment-sales ratio
Intel	127.40	1	5%	563.13	1	7%	22.4%
Qualcomm	51.09	2	–7%	154.36	4	–4%	33.1%
Broadcom	31.88	3	–4%	153.32	5	1%	20.5%
Samsung	28.81	4	11%	435.35	2	4%	6.5%
Toshiba	27.77	5	–5%	109.22	9	16%	27.6%
TSMC	22.15	6	7%	293.24	3	11%	7.5%
Mediatek	17.30	7	13%	86.10	11	29%	20.2%
Micron	16.81	8	5%	128.42	7	–11%	11.1%
NXP	15.60	9	–6%	94.98	10	–10%	16.4%
SK Hynix	15.14	10	9%	142.34	6	–15%	10.2%
NVIDIA	14.63	11	10%	63.4	16	35%	22%
Texas Instrument	13.70	12	7%	123.49	8	2%	11%
STMicro	13.36	13	–6%	69.44	13	1%	19.3%

(2) An entrenched industrial establishment

Since investment is so critical in semiconductor development, many companies would pump large amounts of money into the industry to make up for the gap once and for all.

However, in the complicated and globalized semiconductor ecological chain, things are far more than just the simple act of investment. It is actually about the accumulation effect of investment, which is a long process that costs money and time. This accumulation effect can only be realized after a product has gone through many rounds of developing, manufacturing, launching, being tested and criticized in the market, and then improving under a new round of investment. For China's semiconductors to get on a virtuous cycle of investment-induced improvement, it is highly necessary that its products get into a large-scale application which, as has been proved, is rather impossible.

A technical foundation, including technology structure and stand ard, has long been established by industrial leaders like Intel and

Qualcomm, and upon this foundation grows robust tree trunks like Microsoft, Apple and Google, then branches of various hardware and software providers. All of these combine to form an entrenched and sprawling network where newcomers can hardly take up a stronghold. From the ARK series at the beginning of the 21st century to the most recent Loongson series, China's microchips have failed to interconnect with the existing system. The most advanced technology can be beaten by an all-encompassing and all-compatible network, because the latter does not need to develop a whole new set of technical standard and structure. Hu Weiwu, Loongson's CEO, also admitted that the restriction of the current industrial network is as discouraging as the limitation caused by a lack of technology.

The indispensability of trial and error in the process of building up the semiconductor ecosphere must be highlighted again. Take Huawei for example. It is through this process of continuous trial and improvement facilitated by its downstream industrial chain that its self-developed microchips applied in smartphones, once discarded by the market, can improve to achieve a global market share inferior only to Apple and Qualcomm.

In the smartphone industry, Huawei may have set up an encouraging example of forging a stronghold in the formidable market through trial and error. However, when it comes to the market for high-end telecoms equipment, there is no platform for trial and error for Chinese companies. Even most of China's state-owned companies would rather buy from established international giants like Intel and Qualcomm than from domestic Chinese companies who are still in the earlier stage of trial and error process. In the long run, this entrenched industrial establishment would further handicap China's technology development.

(3) Lopsided talent pool

Besides investments and the industrial ecosphere, another foundation that supports the semiconductor industry is qualified scientists and technicians. Unfortunately, they are not so abundant in China. There are more than 2,600 computer-related majors in the Chinese higher education system, but most of them do a better job of teaching students to use computers than to create computers. Currently, there is an over-concentration of qualified personnel in the application field of the IT industry and a lack of top-notch talents in the field of research and development for algorithms and microchips.

This imbalance in IT personnel distribution along the industrial chain is caused by several reasons. First, the nurturing of high-end semiconductor R&D people requires access to top-level technologies, which only a limited number of institutions in China can provide. Second, China's education system has not quite followed up with the pace of China's IT industry development. For example, most institutions' appraisal mechanism is still publication-based, which is not an effective criterion for assessing research performance in the IT industry. This old practice is impairing creativity and innovation.

A third and a more practical reason is that the financial rewards and career prospects of R&D personnel in China's IT industry are not good enough to attract qualified people to work in this field and stay devoted. In a society where the real estate, finance and internet industries are producing stories of fast money nearly every day, where people are increasingly weighted down by rising housing costs, it is easy to understand why IT engineers in China rarely hold on to a specific R&D position for more than 10 years. At the end of the day, it is the paycheck and the returns that determine the flow of talents among different industrial sectors. In companies like IBM and Intel, however, veteran engineers with decades of expertise in a specific technique have become a strong intellectual force and an inspiration for others to follow.

2.3 The US Trump Card

Shortly after the ZTE incident, SMIC felt the pressure to forestall another such crisis and expedited its order of ASML's Extreme Ultraviolet (EUV) Lithography Machine, costing US$120 million and equivalent to the mainland China's largest microchip manufacturer's 2017 annual profit.

It was a sum of money that needed to be spent. Years of bitter experience clearly showed that without the EUV machine produced only by ASML, Chinese companies would not be able to successfully develop the 5 nanometer or even 7 nanometer microchips technique and keep up with world-leading technologies.

The willingness of Chinese companies to pay for the record high price was one thing, the probability of finally sealing the deal was another. After all, US-led export control regulations could easily come in the way. According to the purchase contract between SMIC and ASML, the EUV machine was set to be delivered before 2019, but analysts were not so sure about the final outcome, because the required export certificate still needed the approval of the unpredictable US government.

Just as in the case of ZTE, the US was once again holding in its hands the hegemonic power to exert export control of various dimensions through multiple means upon countries like China.

1. *Long-standing Export Controls*

It all started with the beginning of the Cold War when the Coordinating Committee for Multilateral Export Controls (COCOM) was set up in Paris in November 1949 by the capitalist alliance led by America, England, Japan, France and Australia. The Committee banned its members from exporting tens of thousands of products under the three main categories of military equipment, high-end technology products and other rare commodities to the communist alliance led by the Soviet Union.

Being one of the communist allies, China was put into the list of countries subject to the Committee's export control in 1952. This in effect meant a full-scale blockade on the already backward communist country, making many science projects difficult to carry out. Most of the calculations in China's nuclear experiment during the 1960s were done by hand-operated primitive computer machines because of the unavailability of advanced computers. Although later on computers with an operating speed of 0.1 and even 1 MIPS (million instructions per second) were successfully developed in China, the gap had already been dramatically widened because the US was already in possession of the super computer and the capacity to design and manufacture advanced microchips.

The US Strategy in the Cold War, The Paris Coordinating Committee and the China Committee.

After the end of the Cold War, COCOM lost its raison d'être and was disbanded in 1994. The end of the Committee did not spell the end of the export control. Shortly afterwards, COCOM's successor, the Wassenaar Arrangement came into being.

The Wassenaar Arrangement on Export Controls for Conventional Arms and Dual-Use Goods and Technologies is an international treaty established in 1996 by the world's main industrial equipment and arms manufacturers. It aims to restraint and regulate the international trade and exchange of conventional arms and strategic technologies. The Arrangement is signed off by 33 member countries, 17 of which are old members of COCOM.

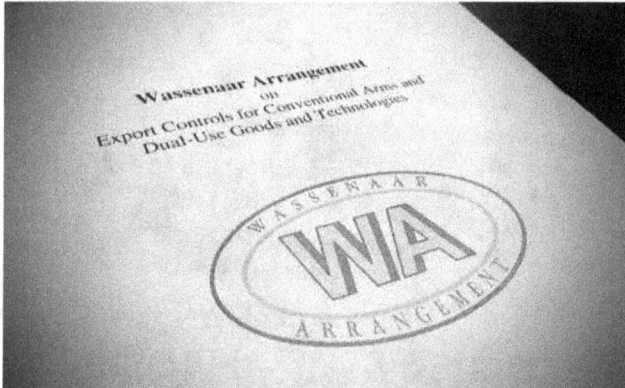

The Wassenaar Arrangement.

There are two lists of objects subject to the export control of the Arrangement: one is a list of dual-use (military and civil) goods and technologies covering nine categories including advanced material, electronics components, computers, material treatment techniques, telecoms and information security, sensors and lasers, navigators and electronic devices for aerospace, watercraft and maritime devices, and propelling systems. The other is a list of conventional arms including 22 categories of weapons, ammunition, warfare devices and warring platforms.

China is again among the list of countries under the new export control. Although there is active cooperation between China and the US in fields like energy, environment and sustainable development, there is little intersection between the two countries in sensitive hi-tech fields like aeronautics and astronautics.

Semiconductors is another field where strict export control has been implemented. Products from advanced manufacturing equipment to microchips used for high-accuracy digital devices are banned from being exported to China.

According to the 2017 US National Security Strategy published by the Trump administration at the end of the year, the US government would take further steps including tightening up on its visa procedures to make sure that its intellectual property would not be acquired by or transferred to its competitors in other parts of the world. Five months later, news came from the US State Department that new visa regulations had been issued to relevant embassies and consulates around the world, and that one of them was a one-year visa restriction on any Chinese students studying in American universities in certain high-tech majors including robotics, aerospace and intelligent manufacturing.

Although it was later confirmed by the State Department that there was no tightening-up on Chinese students' visa application, many US top universities frankly spoke of a high probability that the US government would control the number of Chinese students studying high-tech majors in US universities through stricter censorship on their visa application.

2. *More Than Just Export Control*

The mysterious Malaysia Airline MH370 incident in 2014 brought a quite unexpected news that Rolls Royce, a world-leading aircraft engine manufacturer, continued to monitor its engines even after they were sold, so as to acquire technical information like rotating rates, temperatures, working hours and locations. The news revealed how upstream companies with core technologies like Rolls Royce could impose their own will on the most strategic resources in the 21st century, that is, information resources.

Self-developed and controllable technologies are not 100% secure, but imported and uncontrollable technologies are 100% insecure, as said by Ni Guangnan, a CAE academician who specializes in semiconductors. He believed that it is true in every high-tech industry, and he warned that dependence on others for core technologies would impose great danger not only on supply chain security but also on China's national security.

There had been a series of such lessons around the world. In February 2011, Iran abruptly decided to discharge all the nuclear fuel from its Bushehr nuclear power plant, where high-profile and ambitious nuclear experiments were carried out. The US Secretary of State Hillary Clinton responded quickly by announcing that Iran's nuclear program had been put on a delay. Shortly before this, there were grave concerns that Iran would make its own atomic weapons within a year.

Details published later showed that 1/5 of the Bushehr plant's centrifugal machines were suddenly out of work, and Iran's nuclear research was subsequently paused for at least two years. The lingering question was why the otherwise qualified centrifugal machines broke down immediately after they were put into operation? New machines were dragged into the plant one after another, but none of them would work.

Iran's Bushehr nuclear power plant.

Were it not for a disclosure report by the *New York Times* one year later, we would not have known what had happened in the Bushehr plant. It turned out that Iran's nuclear plant was a victim of a highly contentious and complicated worm virus called Stuxnet. The virus sneaked into Bushehr's monitoring program and stole control of the station's core devices, which enabled it to mislead the operation of the cooling system and the turbine motors so as to cause the centrifugal machines to be disrupted and then entered a self-destruction process. All these had been done secretly behind Iran's back.

Different from the traditional concept of internet viruses aimed at manipulating software, Stuxnet can effectively tamper with the actual physical world by hacking into the internet, working like an missile. It can be targeted at real world infrastructure like pipelines, power plants, telecommunication facilities and airport facilities. After a decompilation of the extremely sophisticated virus, internet security experts asserted that Stuxnet could not have been developed by some unorganized hackers but had to be the product of a group of highly-coordinated experts with a state-level sponsorship.

The report revealed a secret internet program codenamed Olympic Games initiated by the US government since 2006 to handicap Iran's nuclear program. Stuxnet might well have been one of the results of the program and a product co-developed by the US and Israel, who took advantage of the loopholes existing in the monitoring programs of some industrial infrastructures and created an internet virus that could hide itself and also spread itself through storage disks and internet connection.

Apart from retaliating against those countries from the opposing side, such as Iran, the US also took secret actions towards its allies with the help of its dominating telecoms technologies, as revealed by the PRISM program.

The PRISM program, disclosed in June 2013, shocked the world as it showed that the US National Security Agency (NSA) had nearly the whole world under its surveillance and monitoring by ordering US internet giants including Google, Yahoo, Microsoft and Apple to connect their backstage servers to the NSA information storage system. Countries under surveillance even included those whom the US claimed to be close allies with, like England, Germany and Australia. If German

Chancellor Angela Merkel's private phone was watched by the US, countries like China that were viewed as US rivals would be all the more targeted for close surveillance.

At the beginning of 2018, we were again taken aback by the discovery of two 20-year-old security loopholes that existed in the processor microchips produced by international giants like Intel. Named Meltdown and Spectre, the loopholes could enable internet hackers to distant-control the computer system and acquire data and information. The affected devices were on a worldwide basis, from personal and institutional computers, smartphones to cloud computing servers. Although there is no evidence so far to show that these two loopholes have been exploited maliciously, potentially devastating risks exist all the time.

China's President Xi Jinping has repeatedly emphasized the strategic significance of accelerating technological innovation, especially mastering core technologies. He stressed that if core technologies continue to be controlled by others, they will greatly endanger China's national development. Xi highlighted on many occasions that to master these fate-determining technologies, China has only its own strength and efforts to depend on, thererby emphasizing China's aspiration and urgency to develop its own pivotal technologies.

2.4 Core Technology: Must Realize Self-dependency

Steve Jobs, the founder of Apple, was known for his obsessive devotion to his job in the neighborhood of Silicon Valley. He called his iPhone designers at 2:00 am just to spell out his demand of having nickel screw in the iPhone instead of having stainless steel ones. This obsession is still part of Apple today, even though Jobs had left his Mothership forever. For example, Apple's charge technology only allows original Apple Store-bought cables to charge its iPhones, and any cheap copy or unrecognized cable will be rejected.

Apple's charging cable is more than what meets the eye.

Chip researchers' study of Apple's Lightning Cable found an astonishing 4 chips in the tiny pocket area of its lightning port connecting to the phone. One of the most complicated chips has 5,000 logic gates, 128 bit storage capacity, integrated drive transistors, analog circuit and large amount of capacitance, resembling the look of a miniature city under the microscope. Everything required by a communication chip can be found in it.

Apple's Lightning Cable.

Research also showed that the chip, made by the chip giant Texas Instruments, is the pivotal part of Apple's Lightning Cable. Being able to identify each other through code signals, the cable and Apple's devices work together to make sure that any unauthorized cable would be refused by an automatic disconnect.

Thanks to that, Apple can bid a safe farewell to pirated data cable — only cables with MFi license can be accepted into working with Apple devices. For a company to apply for this MFi license, it must have a self-owned factory with an area of no less than 2,000 square meters and a workforce of no less than 50 employees. It also has to pay a franchise fee of US$8,500 and put in several months of design and redesign until everything meets Apple's standard. Finally, for those who are lucky enough to land themselves the MFi license, they have to purchase this aforementioned chip, sold at US$2.00, through Apple's designated franchisers.

For sure, all the manufacturing costs find their way into the selling price. A one-meter USB-C to Lightning Cable is sold at US$19.00 in the Apple Store.

Four chips in a single Lightning connector. We can only imagine there are way more in the whole device, which can include but are not confined to communication baseband chips, Wi-Fi chips, memory chips and fingerprint identification chips. Each type of these chips is dominated in the market by a certain manufacturer. For example, Qualcomm takes up half the market share for baseband chips and Broadcom leads the market for Wi-Fi chips and RF front chips, while Samsung has long been defining the industry of memory chips.

Industry insiders revealed that more than 50% of the communication baseband main chips used in the Chinese Android smartphone market is from foreign suppliers. Huawei, Xiaomi, OPPO and Vivo, as leading Chinese smartphone brands, import large numbers of baseband chips from abroad. Among the four of them, Huawei has self-developed baseband chips, but its RF front chips and memory chips are mostly imported from overseas chip giants.

Chips with the size of a fingernail can be so high-end and technology-steeped that Xiaomi's CEO Lei Jun called them the most intricate and complicated object on earth due to their extra-high demand for stability so as to accommodate different component modules required in a smartphone.

Lack of self-sustained chips is inflicting losses in the Chinese smartphone industry. With Chinese brands rising up to the mid-range and high-end markets, the increased import costs for upmarket subassembly components is going to eat into the profit of its smartphone industry. Yet the big problem is, researching and developing chips requires more than ambition and determination.

1. *Foxconn Besieged*

You may still remember Foxconn's ambition for an industry transformation, but global acquisition does not always work smoothly for the King of Outsourcing. After its successful acquisition of Sharp, which took two years of strenuous efforts, Foxconn had its eyes set on Toshiba, a Japanese company as influential and long-standing as HP, for its flash memory chips business. However, this time, Foxconn was faced with a determined opposing force and a more tedious fight.

As a prestigious player in the global semiconductor industry, Toshiba possesses a good number of advanced technologies and is the world's second largest (topped by Samsung) producer of flash memory chips, a kind of storage chip widely applied in personal computers and smartphones.

Burdened by the underperformance of some of its business sectors, Toshiba's financial condition worsened and was forced to put up its microchips asset for sale in order to transfuse blood into its parent company. As soon as the offer came out, three of the world's largest semiconductor conglomerates started to compete for Toshiba's flash memory business. They were Foxconn from China, Broadcom from the US and a consortium representing US, Japanese and Korean interests, including Japanese Development Bank (JDB), the Innovation Network Corporation of Japan (INCJ) and other semiconductors companies.

With the united support of its important partners including hi-tech giants Amazon and Apple, Foxconn offered a price of US$27 billion to Toshiba. In order to remove the misgivings the Japanese government had about Toshiba's core technologies getting leaked, Foxconn assured that the acquisition was an independent and uninfluenced decision of its own and promised an autonomous operation and management for the Japanese company. Guo Taiming also made the point that his company, responsible for producing more than half of the world's most popular electronic devices, would lend itself well to cooperate with Toshiba to develop storage devices that meet customer demands.

The Japanese side, however, was determined to prevent any transactions that would run the risks of transferring Toshiba's core technologies to foreign countries. There was a concern by the Japanese government that Foxconn's successful acquisition of Toshiba might well mean a technology leakage to China.

Japan was straightforward and candid in 2016 during the Chinese company's acquisition of Sharp. Guo recalled in a press conference that he was warned by Japan's Ministry of Economy, Trade and Industry to withdraw from the acquisition procedure of Sharp, otherwise the influence of

INCJ, a foundation backed by the Japanese government might be introduced into the scene. Guo's first response was, "Am I being threatened or am I being ordered?" The whole episode left a sour note for some time.

2. A Major Setback

In the end, though, Sharp was successfully acquired by Foxconn. However, in the Toshiba case which was influenced by both INCJ and JDB, Foxconn was not so successful. In June 2017, Foxconn's acquisition application for Toshiba was officially rejected by Toshiba.

In a forum held in Beijing shortly after the ZTE incident, there were several critical voices about China's semiconductor industry. In Li Guojie's speech, he regarded the development of a country's semiconductors, which required a lengthy and deep accumulation across the entire industrial chain from raw material, production equipment to designing and manufacturing, to be representative of a country's overall national strength. Money alone could not make up for the gap in this industry, he said.

In Bao Yungang's view, the widening of the technology gap between China and the US to its largest extent was because China missed out on the golden age of the semiconductor industry back in the 1970s and 1980s. Bao, an academician from the Institute of Computer Technology (ICT) under the CAS, noted that the development of every category of microchips was the result of tens of thousands of engineers, designers and researchers' long-time effort and devotion in the last half century.

Loongson's CEO Hu Weiwu exclaimed at the unexpectedness of America's move and reckoned that if the export restriction took place five years later, it would be much easier for China to cope with the tough situation.

Besides the aforementioned forum, many other people were also reflecting on what had happened to China's semiconductor industry.

Ma Yun, founder of Alibaba, said in his keynote address in the first Digital China Summit in 22th April 2018 that core technologies were what really counted, and that leading companies in China should take on the responsibility to innovate and break new grounds in the industry if they wanted to maintain their leadership.

Ma Huateng, CEO and founder of Tencent, described the ZTE incident as a wake-up call that pushed China to accelerate its semiconductor industry with unprecedented urgency.

Liu Qiangdong, CEO and founder of Jingdong, highlighted that the ZTE incident was not just about one company, instead it was a slap on the face of every Chinese IT company. He added that China should draw critical lessons from this incident, that is, if the country did not grow stronger by creating its own IP, its fate would always be determined by others.

Prior to all these sanctions and restrictions started by the US, the global IT industry had been a fertile land in which free market dominated and globalization value prevailed. Although the risks had been forewarned, few would believe that America, the pioneer of market economy and globalization, would indeed adopt a politicized approach to interfere with market operations.

The severe and awakening effect of the ZTE incident on China's semiconductor industry was bitterly reminiscent of the US bombing of the Chinese Embassy in Yugoslavia in 1999. Ren Zhengfei, the founder and CEO of Huawei, pointed out that China should be strategic in its quest and bid for the overlap of the technology curve and the demand curve in order to be ready for counteraction.

2.5 Lack of Self-dependency: Not Only in Semiconductors

An important lesson learned from the ZTE incident is that China and nearly all the major hi-tech companies in China are highly dependent on US technologies for their existence. ZTE and Huawei, BATX (Baidu, Alibaba, Tencent, Xiaomi), Didi (China's Uber), and some of the largest Chinese companies including Industrial and Commercial Bank of China, Bank of China, China Mobile, China Telecom, PetroChina and SAIC Motor all rely in some way or another on technologies, components, software and intellectual properties from many American companies like Apple, 3M, AMD, Applied Materials, Cisco, Corning, Google, Intel, Micron, Microsoft, Qualcomm, Seagate and Western Digital.

Value of China's imported advanced goods (billion US$).

Value of China's imported advanced goods	year	2013	2014	2015	2016	2017
Across sectors		19243	19593	16752	15802	19151
Integrated circuit		2313	2176	2307	2271	2601
Hi-end medical equipment		150	158	173	184	204
Digital control tool machine		40	35	30	26	29

A ban on the sale of American technologies to China is bad enough to the Chinese economy. Looking at the current state of the US-China trade dispute, it is not too far off to imagine that if the US decides to extend the American technology ban to other — or all — Chinese firms, the entire Chinese economy could be brought to its knees.

While the US has a strategic edge that China cannot easily counter, it may not last. By threatening the future of one of China's most important international companies, the Trump administration has likely prodded China to redouble its efforts to close that crucial technological gap and end its dependency on Western technology. What's more, the US move would spur the creation of new competitors in the industry whom China could seek out for alternative supply. Plus, there is a big concern that the export restriction on American companies from selling to China would eat away a big proportion of their profit margins.

Stephen Roach, former chairman of Morgan Stanley Asia and the firm's chief economist, said that the China bashing was more an outgrowth of US domestic problems than a response to a genuine external threat. It is true, in the sense that the accusations alleged in the "301 investigation" report, including the US$600 billion economic toll caused by China's infringement of IPR and the trade deficit with China, are false or at least unconfirmed narrative. Instead, they are caused by the macroeconomic imbalances of the US' own making and the fear of the consequences of US retreat from global leadership.

An article published right after the ZTE incident in *People's Daily*, the official newspaper of the Central Committee of the Communist

Party of China, stated that the Chinese government's and the Chinese people's stance towards the US blow is one of cautious optimism. It said, "We won't panic and lose confidence that China is capable of finding a way out just like it had before. At the same time, we won't lose sight of the fact that a win-win relationship with the rest of the world and a deepening of the opening-up policy are the principles to be upheld in China's strategy-making."

References

1. Akio Morita & Shintaro Ishihara. *The Japan That Can Say No: Why Japan Will Be First Among Equals* [M]. 1989.
2. Yin Sheng. *Against the Tide: ZTE's Rise in the Winter of the Industry* [M]. Beijing: China Citic Press. 2010.
3. Walter Isaacson. *Steve Jobs*. 2011.
4. Cui Pi. *American Containment Strategies and COCOM, CHINCOM*. Zhonghua Book Company. 2005.
5. Hou Yuhong. *The Origin and Development of the Wassenaar Arrangement* [J]. International Forum. 2005.
6. Li Zheng. *Independent Development in Microchips is Indispensable for China to Prosper*. People's Daily. 2018.

Chapter 3

A Close-up on Microchips

Overture

The most crucial component in today's omnipresent and "omnipotent" electronic devices are the omnipresent and "omnipotent" microchips, the protagonist in this book.

Although microchips have become indispensable to human beings, most people are actually unacquainted with microchips.

In a highly specialized global industrial chain necessitated by the sophisticated nature of microchips fabrication, there is not a single company nor even a single country who can undertake the entire chain on its own.

From inconspicuous grains of silicon sands to square-millimeters-sized microchips which are capable of conjuring the most delicate and unimaginable digital magic, what is the incredible journey behind the scene?

From the designing process to the foundry of wafer using monocrystalline silicon to the photolithography fabrication and packaging, what are the secrets behind each of these exquisite technical processes?

> Supposing the minimum component costs stay the same, the number of transistors in a dense integrated circuit doubles about every 18 months, and so does the performance of the integrated circuit.
>
> — Gordon Moore, Co-founder of Intel

3.1 Microchips on the World's Stage

Hi-tech electronic devices that are rapidly evolving and becoming increasingly sophisticated have never ceased to impress and amaze people since the advent of the Information Age. Weaving magic inside these electronics are integrated circuits, or microchips, made from silicon. Microchips have become the building blocks of electronic devices.

ENIAC, the world's first general-purpose electronic computer made in 1946, looks like a grotesque and alien giant to today's eyes.

The whole computer weighed more than 30 tons and occupied an area more than 170 square meters and had indicator lights, electronic meters and wires crawling all over its surface. Scientists installed 18,000 electronic vacuum tubes, thousands of diodes, resistors and other electronic components into ENIAC, and there were more than 500,000 soldering points. It was said that the machine needed 174 kilowatts of electricity per hour. An interesting story about the ENIAC was that every time it was turned on for calculating purposes, the whole Pennsylvania University Town's lights would fade out. When operating the device, quite a few experienced technicians needed to be in attendance, including one just to take care of the electronic tubes among which at least one would break down every 15 minutes.

Despite all that, or maybe because of all that, ENIAC became the most advanced calculator then, with a computing rate 200,000 times faster than manual calculation and 1,000 times faster than the old relay computing machine. The successful development of such a computing device boded well for the project sponsor, the American Army who was then in an urgency to develop new ballistic missiles in order to deter the Axis powers in World War II. It took ENIAC only three fleeting seconds to complete a calculation on ballistic trajectory, which used to take two hundred people two months to finish.

The secret in this jaw-dropping leap in large-scale calculation capacity was the hundreds of thousands of vacuum tubes installed in ENIAC. However, the obstacle in achieving an even faster computing speed lied in the punched cardboard storage system which was space-consuming and slow in operation. Since then, there was a race to scale down and speed up ENIAC-like computing devices.

The world's first general-purpose electronic computing machine, ENIAC.

In the history of science and technology development, it has been proven repeatedly that a tireless technological pursuit is the perfect impetus for scientific breakthrough. After the birth of ENIAC, the search for quicker and smaller computers drove scientists to look for vacuum tubes that were more stable and space-saving and storage systems that were more intelligent.

Transistors, the fundamental building blocks for all electronic devices, were invented in the Alcatel-Lucent Bell Labs in 1947. Transistors were able to make up for the shortcomings of vacuum tubes in size, power consumption and service life. It heralded the invention of integrated circuitry which greatly boosted the progress of military science, aeronautics and space research, and of course modern computer development.

However, problems started to crop up when circuitry network had to expand to meet higher functional needs and the components needed for the circuitry not only increased in number but also in size. Scientists were again beset with the problem of how to further cut down the size of electronic components like transistors to save costs.

The very first integrated circuitry was created by Jack Kilby from Texas Instruments in 1958, before the advent of the Information Age that swept the whole world in the latter half of the 20th century. Thanks to this invention, computers have gone from as large as a house at their first debut to hand-portable nowadays. Not just computers, integrated circuits or microchips have also propelled the development of the human race as a whole and became omnipresent in the everyday life of human society.

The electronic alarm clock that wakes us up every morning with its sweet music will not go off at the right time if not for the control by microchips. The LED table lamp at our bedside will not illuminate if not for the microchips that stabilize the voltage. When we make phone calls or send messages or use other functions of a smartphone, several microchips are working at full capacity simultaneously. When we enjoy the pleasure of cooking in the kitchen, microchips are running our refrigerator, microwave oven and other electronic appliances to make sure everything is at our service. From household devices to industrial numerical control machines to national defense missiles, satellites, rockets and warships, microchips are ubiquitous, as far as our eyes can see and as deep as our minds can imagine.

1. *Naming Microchips*

When we talk about microchips, we want to think of it as a miniature structure of an all-incorporated and fully-functional circuitry on the surface of a tiny silicon substrate packaged inside a protective case. On the surface of the silicon wafer, a large number (about billions) of electronic components including transistors, diodes, resistors, capacitances and inductances are interconnected according to the PCB design to form an integrated circuitry. More than a hundred procedures are needed to complete the integration and packaging process, after which microchips can be rendered smaller than the size of a finger nail.

Besides the more familiar and friendly name of microchip, we also use the terms — integrated circuit (IC) and semiconductor, as seen in the previous chapters. Is there any difference among them, or the three of them can be used interchangeably? To put the matter to rest, we should first know that microchip is another name for integrated circuit and that integrated circuit is one of the four categories of products falling under the realm of the semiconductor industry, with the other three being discrete devices, photoelectric devices and transducers or sensors. Sometimes when we hear semiconductor, we would naturally relate it to integrated circuit because the latter accounts for more than 80% of the whole semiconductor market share.

Microchip the size of a fingernail.

The trickiest and most challenging part in the manufacturing of microchips or integrated circuits is to routinely integrate millions (tens of billions nowadays) of electronic components onto a piece of silicon chip the size of a fingernail.

2. Microchips Family

According to their functions, microchips can further be divided into processor chips, memory and storage chips and chips for particular usages. Microchips used for processing are more widely known as central processing units (CPU), which are commonly embedded into computers, smartphones, tablet personal computers, televisions, refrigerators and other electronic devices to carry out core instructions by performing basic arithmetic, logic, controlling and calculating operations. CPU functions in an electronic device much like how our brain works to carry out our bodily functions. Microchips for memory and storage, as the name suggests, are used to store information and data, typically in computers and smartphones, for immediate use or reprogram. Specific functional chips are also familiar to us. For example, when we want to get connected to a Wi-Fi network or use Bluetooth to share stuff, or when we want a smartphone with more intelligent battery management, specifically designed microchips are running behind the scene to make all of these happen.

Inside Knowledge

Semiconductor Material

All natural and manmade materials can be classified as conductors and non-conductors based on their electrical conductivity or the ability to transmit electricity. Conductors, represented by all types of metal, is able to transmit electricity pretty well. Non-conductors, a poor performer in transmitting electricity, are represented by materials like coal, artificial crystalloid, ceramic, plastic and glass. Then there are semiconductors whose electrical conductivity fall between a metal and an insulator, and whose conducting properties can be altered in useful ways by deliberate and controlled means. The unique behavior of semiconductors forms the basis of diodes, transistors and all the other modern electronics components. Some common semiconductor materials include silicon, germanium and gallium arsenide (GaAs), of which silicon has been the most widely commercialized in the electronics industry.

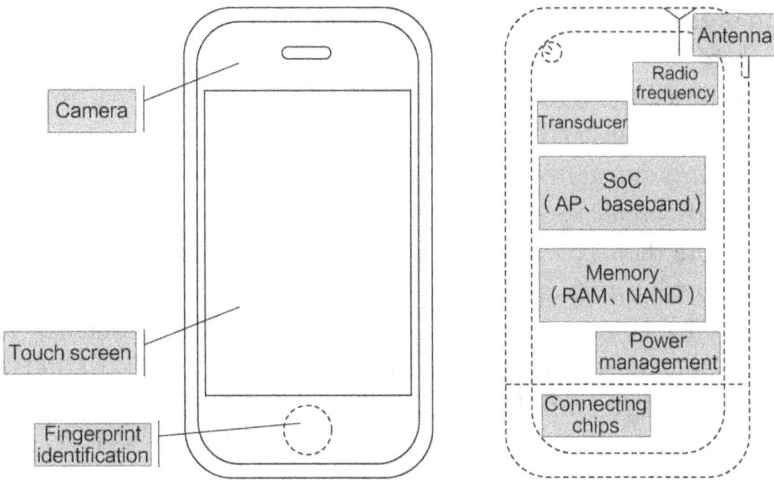

Hardware within a smartphone.

Microchips used in smartphones and their global suppliers.

Microchips used for/in/as	Functions	Main suppliers
SoC (System on a chip)	Integrating AP processor and baseband processor; responsible for logic, signal and protocol processing.	Qualcomm, Apple, Media Tek, Hisilicon, Samsung,
Radio frequency	Receiving and sending radio frequency, synthesizing frequency and amplifying power.	Skyworks, Qorvo, Murata
Memory & storage	Storing information and data.	Samsung, Hynix, Micron, Toshiba
Camera	Transforming optical signals into electronic signals.	Sony, Samsung, Omnivision
Touchscreen	Providing multi-touch control.	Synopsys, FocalTech
Fingerprint identification	Identifying fingerprints.	FPC, Qualcomm, Synopsys, Versuit
Power management	Providing dynamic voltage scaling and dynamic frequency scaling to optimize the power-performance tradeoff.	Qualcomm, MTK, Hynix
Connecting	Providing wireless connection to Wi-Fi or Bluetooth.	Broadcom, Qualcomm

In order for our readers to have a more comprehensive understanding, here are some other methods of classification for microchips. According to the signal sources processed by the circuitry, there are analog microchips and digital microchips. According to the number of components integrated onto a circuitry, there are five categories of microchips: Small Scale Integrated Circuits (SSIC) with an integration of no more than 100 components; Medium Scale Integrated Circuits (MSIC) with an integration of 100–1,000 components; Large Scale Integrated Circuits (LSIC) with 1,000–100,000 components; Very Large Scale Integrated Circuits (VLSIC) with 100,000–10,000,000 components and Ultra Large Scale Integrated Circuits (ULSIC) with 10,000,000 and above components. Microchips used in today's smartphones are all ULSIC with billions of components built within.

3.2 A Short History of Microchips

The transformative arrival of integrated circuits into our lives can be dated back to 1947 when John Bardeen (1908–1991), Walter Brattain (1902–1987) and William Shockley (1910–1989) from the Bell Labs invented transistors. This invention formed the basis for all modern electronic components and triggered the Third Industrial Revolution, which brought forth the new era of the Information Age into human history. In celebration of their great contributions to human society development, the three scientists were granted the 1956 Nobel Prize in Physics.

Then in 1952, the idea of an integrated circuit was first brought up by the British scientist G. W. A. Dummer. Six years later in 1958, Jack Kilby (1923–2005) from Texas Instruments [along with Robert Noyce (1927–1990) from Fairchild Semiconductors] successively invented the first integrated circuit in the world. This pioneering act was a gift to humankind and the milestone it set for modern information technology earned Kilby the 2000 Nobel Prize in Physics. Just as it led the world into the time of integrated circuits more than half a century ago, Texas Instruments still leads the semiconductor industry today.

Jack Kilby invented the first integrated circuit in 1958.

The advantage of integrated circuits is that they can speed up the large-scale commercialization and manufacturing of modern electronics devices. Integrated circuits are small and light, unnoticeable even, which largely cuts down material costs in the manufacturing process. With a considerably long lifespan and a stable operation performance, they have been found to be useful and applicable in every electronical aspect.

The following shows the development history of microchips over a span of 60 years.

Development history of microchips (information from Forward Industry Institute).

Time	Events
1947	Transistors were invented by John Bardeen, Walter Brattain, William Shockley from the Bell Labs.
1958	The first integrated circuit came into being.
1964	Gordon Moore predicted that the number of transistors in integrated circuits would double every 18 months. This observation was known as Moore's Law.
1966	CMOS (Complementary Metal-Oxide Semiconductor) integrated circuits and gate array design were developed by RCA (Radio Corporation of America).
1971	Intel launched the first 1 kilobyte DRAM (Dynamic Random Access Memory) and the first LSIC, the Intel 4004 microprocessor.

(Continued)

(Continued)

Time	Events
1978	The newly developed 64 kilobyte DRAM incorporated 140,000 transistors in a silicon chip with a size no more than 0.5 square centimeter.
1988	1-square-centimeter 16 megabyte DRAM integrated with 35 million transistors was successfully developed, announcing the arrival of VLSIC.
1993	Intel successfully developed its 66 megahertz Pentium processor with 0.6 micrometer technique.
1999	Pentium III processor with a CPU clock rate of 450 megahertz was successfully developed using 0.25 micrometer and then 0.18 micrometer techniques.
2003	Pentium 4E series was developed with 90 nanometer technique.
2009	Intel's Core i series was launched, declaring the arrival of 32 nanometer technique.
2015	IBM successfully developed the 7 nanometer technique.

1. *The First Integrated Circuit Board*

With several crawling wires connecting two or three plain-looking electronic components, the first integrated circuit board, seemingly unhandy, might not look like today's powerful and miniature Intel microprocessors. However, it worked much more efficiently than what the individual parts could ever do.

The first integrated circuit board.

2. *Semiconductor Device-and-lead Structure*

The concept of an integrated circuitry was on the mind of many engineers in the 1950s, but two men actually transformed the idea into a real application. After Kilby designed and made the initial prototype for present-day integrated circuits, as seen in the above picture, Noyce formulated his semiconductor device-and-lead structure which turned out to be one of the fundamental technology bases for the large-scale manufacturing of integrated circuitry. Kilby and Noyce were recognized as the co-inventors of integrated circuit and both of them were awarded the US National Medal of Science. In 1960, Fairchild Semiconductor developed the first commercially used monolithic integrated circuitry which was able to achieve its function independently without external electric connection.

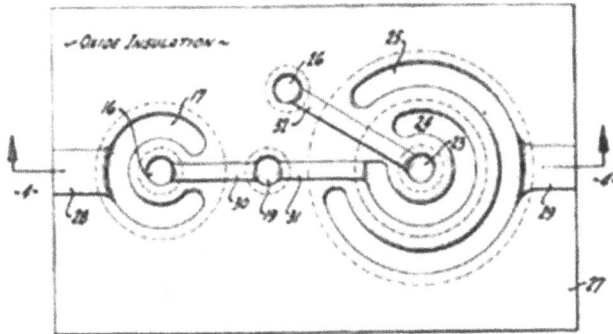

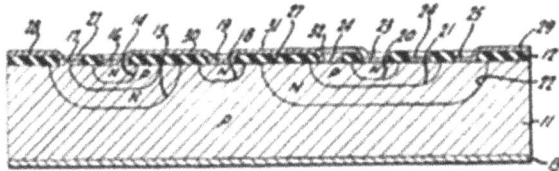

Semiconductor device-and-lead structure.

3. *Molecular Electronic Computer*

With all its apparent advantages in size, efficiency, applicability, service life and power consumption, integrated circuit was first widely applied to military devices and the space cause years before it was brought into the civil industry department. In 1961, Texas Instruments developed the first IC-based computer, called molecular electronic computer, under the commission of the US Air Force. After that, the National Aeronautics and Space Administration (NASA) started to show great interest in the technology. Its Apollo Guidance Computer and inter-planetary probe had all been developed based on IC technology.

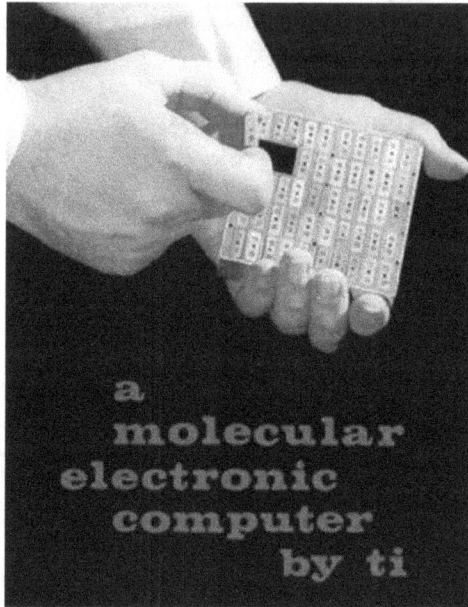

The molecular electronic computer.

4. *Integrated Circuitry Applied to Missile Guidance System*

In 1962, Texas Instruments developed 22 sets of integrated circuitry for the missile guidance systems of Minuteman I and Minuteman II, which marked the beginning of the application of integrated circuitry in missile guidance systems. By the year 1965, the US Air Force had surpassed NASA to become the world's largest consumer of integrated circuitry.

Integrated circuitry applied to the missile guidance system.

5. *Moore's Law*

Gordon Moore, co-founder of Intel, made a unique contribution to the development of the semiconductor industry as an electronics engineer. He was known for his prediction in 1965 that the number of components in a dense integrated circuit would continue to double approximately every 18 months and that by 1975 the number of components integrated onto a piece of microchip would reach 65,000. This calculation, known as Moore's Law, was a target of miniaturization in the semiconductor industry for many years and heralded many technical changes.

Co-founder of Intel, Gordon Moore.

6. *Busicom 141-PF Calculator*

Remember ENIAC and scientists' endeavors to miniaturize giant computing machines during the 1950s and 1960s? It turned out that integrated circuitry was the answer scientists had been searching for to achieve that dream. In 1969, Japan's Nippon Calculating Machine Corporation asked Intel to design a set of integrated circuits for its new line of programmable electronic calculators, which spurred the invention and commercialization of Intel's first microprocessor, the Intel 4004. The electronic calculator thus developed became the first calculator with a microprocessor. It was called Busicom 141-PF.

7. *Intel 4004 Microprocessor*

Designed and built as a custom chip for Nippon Calculating Machine Corporation, Intel 4004 was the first commercially available (sold as a component) microprocessor released by the microchip giant Intel and the first in a long line of Intel CPUs. It heralded a new era in integrated electronics by using the then-new silicon gate technology.

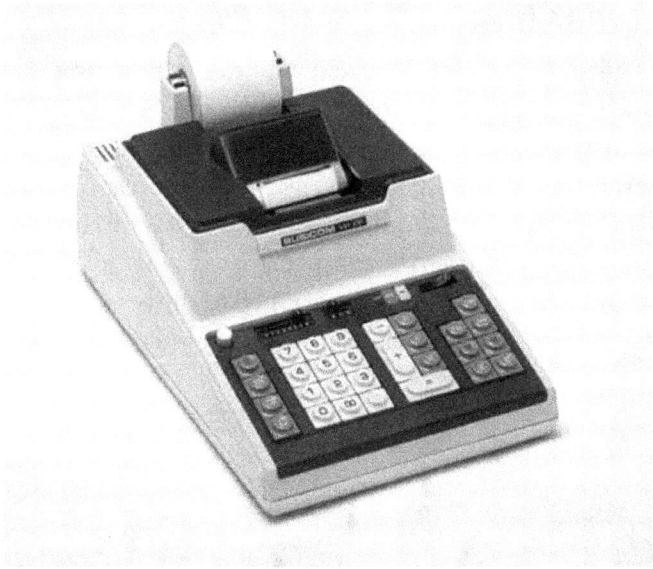

Busicom 141-PF calculator.

Intel 4004 microprocessor.

8. *The World's First Digital Watch, Pulsar*

Pulsar, designed as the world's newest way to tell time, was developed by a team led by John Bergey from Hamilton Watch in 1971. It was among the first few commercial applications of miniaturized integrated circuits. It was feted as a fashion item by the public just as we welcome the launch of new Apple products today. When Pulsar was first launched, it was sold at US$2,100, even more expensive than Hamilton's mechanical series. Now, digital watches have dropped to the bottom of the pyramid among many other products derived from integrated circuitry.

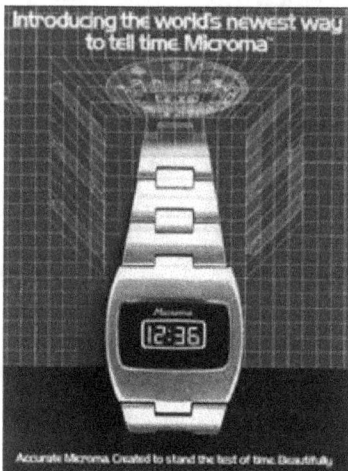

The world's first digital watch, Pulsar.

9. *Nanometer Technique: Transistors Measured in Nanometers*

Can you imagine 30 million of 45 nanometer transistors all packed within the space of the point of a needle? Then think about how many transistors can be integrated into the same space with IBM's newly developed 7 nanometer technique? Yes, that is the size of present-day transistors and that is how tremendously complex integrated circuits have become, a scale even the term ULSIC is not enough to describe. With its size scaled down by tens of millions of times, the cost of a single transistor has decreased to a millionth of its original cost in 1968.

IC technique has advanced in leaps and bounds.

Extra

Microchips Used in the Apollo Guidance Computer Are Not More Advanced Than Chips Used in a Modern Calculator

On 16th July 1969, more than a million people gathered around the Kennedy Space Center located in Florida and another 600 million people around the world watched the live broadcast on their TVs. This was the day that witnessed the realization of a dream that accompanied our civilization from the day humans could think; the first time in our history that we finally breached the earth's gravitation and set foot on the moon.

Neil Armstrong, the commander of Apollo 11, became the first human being to walk on the moon. What he said as he was about to let go of the handrail of the stepladder that connected to the surface of the moon and plant his foot on the moon still echoes today — "That's one small step for a man, one giant leap for mankind".

Many would think that a project as complex and mind-boggling as sending astronauts to the moon in a spacecraft certainly demanded the same complex and mind-boggling calculating capacities for the orbit route, numerous controls and designing instructions. In that respect, many would wonder if human beings were really capable of reaching the moon in 1969 when LSIC was not yet developed until two years later.

It is true that compared with modern-day computers' processing ability, microchips used in the computing system of Apollo 11 to command or assist commanding of the spacecraft were rather primitive. As Jack Garman, one of the computing engineers of the Apollo 11 mission recalled, monitoring devices and real-time screens filled the whole center room of ground control, but their total processing capacity was no better than that of a modern computer. As to the guidance computer that landed Apollo 11 on the moon, it had only 2 megahertz of processing power, 4 kilobyte of RAM, and 72 kilobyte of ROM, less than that of a modern calculator.

However, what many people do not know is that microchips used in space-ships depend not so much on their processing capacity than on their operation stability. Over-heating in one component of the spacecraft or a wrong instruction to one abnormal situation could cause devastating results. It is because spaceships demand and depend on stability, hence it is better to tailor separate microchips for different purposes and different occasions. This is very different from personal computers or smartphones where microchips are designed to execute multiple tasks at the same time. Thus, it is not surprising that the processing capacity of the CPU of the most advanced and recent Mars Curiosity Rover cannot be compared to that of a personal computer ten years ago.

If the CPU of a modern calculator or an outdated non-smartphone is as powerful as or more capable than the whole computing and controlling system of Apollo 11 and its ground control center, then imagine how the exploding progress of microprocessors during the last several decades has propelled today's smartphones. It is possible that any smartphone nowadays has a processing capacity enough to command thousands of Apollo 11 to land on the moon at the same time.

3.3 The Process of IC Fabrication

From natural grains of sands to technology-rich microchips, it is a transformation that goes through hundreds of industrial procedures. In this section, we will take a closer look at the secrets behind the magic transformation of sands into electronic brains.

1. *From Sands to Monocrystalline Silicon Boule*

We have already known that the most widely used semiconductor material to make microchips is silicon. Its most common compound, silicon dioxide ($SiO2$), takes the form of ordinary sand. The silicon that is used for microchips must have a purity close to 100%, that is, no more than one impure atom among one million silicon atoms. To achieve that nearly defect-free purity, it is imperative to perform multiple refinement treatment on the silicon raw material.

In the refinement process, a cylindrical ingot of high purity monocrystalline silicon is formed by pulling a seed crystal from a melt of polysilicon. The single crystal ingot, also called the boule, weighs about 100 kilogram and can achieve a 99.999999% silicon purity.

From sands to the single silicon boule.

2. *Wafer*

The boule is then sliced with a wafer saw and polished to form wafers. Wafer serves as the substrate for microelectronic components to be built into fabricate integrated circuits.

From the boule to wafer.

Inside Knowledge

More about Wafer

You may have come across 12 inch wafer foundry factory when reading news about microchips. What is wafer and what does 12 inch indicate?

Wafer is the substrate for the building of microchips. To put it figuratively, we can compare the fabrication of integrated circuits, with all that designing and engineering, to the construction of a large building again. Just like a building needs a groundwork, the building of microchips needs its groundwork too, and that is where wafers come in.

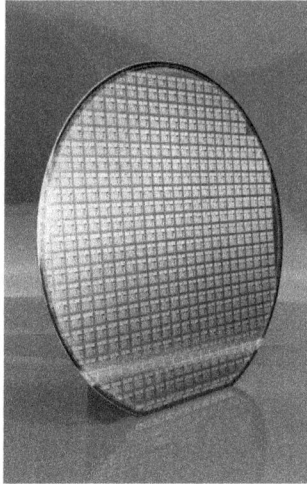

Silicon wafer.

Most of the commercially available wafers nowadays are sliced and polished from the cylindrical monocrystalline silicon boule formed through the crystal pulling process.

Twelve inch actually indicates the diameter of wafers. A bigger number means a larger slice of wafer and a larger slice means more microchips are produced on each slice. However, it is not technically easy to make slices with bigger size, so the mainstream size of wafers for the semiconductor industry is 12 inch, or 300 millimeter.

3. *Photolithography*

Photolithography is a process that uses light to transfer a geometric pattern from a photomask to a photosensitive photoresist on the surface of a wafer substrate. During the photolithography process, a wafer is first covered with a thin and flat layer of photoresist by spin-coating which could remove all the bump or ridge of the resist thus leaving a very flat layer. Photoresist includes positive resist and negative resist, with the former being the most common one.

Photolithography.

Then a patterned mask is applied to the surface of the photoresist to block light, so that only unmasked regions of the resist would be exposed to light. A solvent, called a developer, is then applied to the surface. In the case of a positive photoresist, the exposed part is degraded by light and becomes soluble to the developer, while in the case of a negative photoresist, the exposed part is strengthened by light thus making the unexposed part soluble to the developer. In either case, the developer will dissolve away the soluble part of the photoresist thus leaving behind a coating. The process shares some fundamental principles with photography in that the pattern is created by exposure to light.

Inside Knowledge

Photolithography

We have basically introduced the working mechanism of photolithography, but why do we need to pattern the wafer surface?

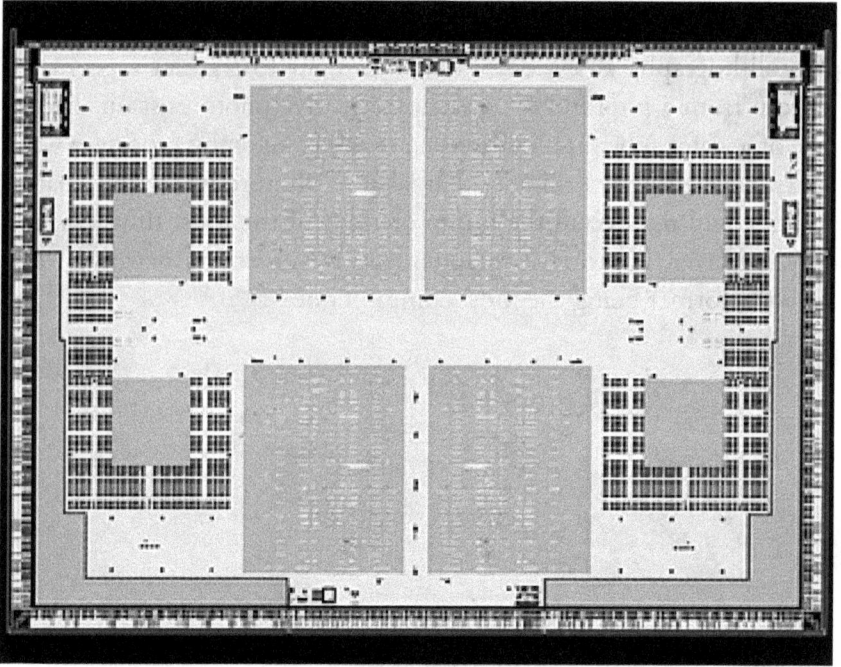

The pattern for Loongson 3A3000.

Remember that wafer is the groundwork for the fabrication of integrated circuits and that integrated circuits are composed of many overlapping layers of micro components? The photolithography procedure is like a repeated printing (or more like etching actually) process based on the PCB design that defines the overlapping layers, with some layers marking where various dopants are diffused into the substrate (called diffusion layers), some define where additional ions are implanted (implant layers), some define the conductors (doped polysilicon or metal layers), and some define the connections between the conducting layers (via or contact layers). All the IC electronic components are constructed from a specific combination of these layers. For example, a transistor is formed wherever the gate layer (polysilicon or metal layer) crosses a diffusion layer.

This method can create extremely small patterns, down to a few tens of nanometers in size. For some complex integrated circuits design, a wafer needs to go through the lithography process as many as 50 times.

4. Die Saw Process

After the photolithography process in which integrated circuits are produced in large patches on a single wafer, the wafer will be cut or diced to many pieces, each containing one copy of the circuit. Each of these pieces is called a die, the unit of a given fabricated functional circuitry, and each is going to be packaged in the following procedure and to be embedded into various electronic devices.

Wafer under cutting.

Dies after cutting.

5. IC packaging

Integrated circuits packaging is the final stage of semiconductor device fabrication, in which the block of semiconductor material is encapsulated in a supporting case that prevents physical damage and corrosion.

Integrated circuits packaging.

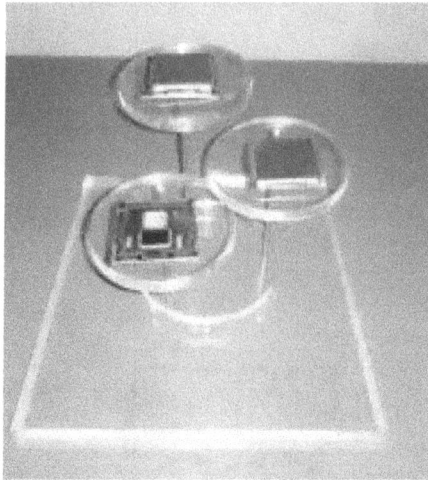

Packaged integrated circuits.

Inside Knowledge

IC Packaging

Being so delicate with a whole labyrinth of nanometer-sized components on it, microchips can easily get scratched or damaged without protection measures, and that is where packaging comes in.

IC packaging needs to take electrical, mechanical and thermal, and economic concerns into consideration. Generally, the packaging process includes die attachment, bonding, encapsulation, and wafer bonding, but not all of these operations are performed for every package since different microchips require different package types.

In order to improve the electrical performance of the package, it is best to keep it as small as possible and at the same time allow for better heat transfer and dissipation. Packaging design has gone through a series of updating. Recent developments consist of stacking multiple dies in a single package, called SiP (System in Package) or multi-chip package, which enables a smaller package case and a speed-up in its operation performance.

A complete functional unit can be built in a multi-chip package, so that few external components need to be added to make it work. Despite this benefit, SiP technique decreases the yield of fabrication since any defective chip in the package will result in a non-functional packaged integrated circuit, even if all other chips in that same package are functional.

The packaging procedure is followed by testing, which is designed to make sure the full functionality of each packaged product and to sift out non-functional ones. After this last process, the qualified final products come off the production line to be sent to customers for the assembly of all kinds of electronic products seen in our daily lives.

Extra

Four Highly Demanding Elements in the IC Fabrication Process

IC fabrication is among the most advanced and demanding manufacturing processes in the world. The following elements are strictly-controlled and indispensable prerequisites in the IC fabrication process.

1. *Cleanroom. The fabrication of integrated circuits demands a strict standard of cleanliness which is quantified by the number of particulates such as dust, airborne organisms, or vaporized particles per cubic meter. In an ISO 1 cleanroom, no particles bigger than 0.3 micrometer are permitted and just 12 particles in the size range of 0.3 micrometer and smaller can be allowed. In a production line where the exquisite fabrication is conducted in a micro world, even one smallest particulate would interfere with the conductivity of nanometer-sized components and cause product*

defect. The users of the cleanroom are the biggest sources of particles contamination, so treatment like air shower in cleanroom garments is mandatory before they enter the room.

2. *Ultrapure Water (UPW). The consumption of water by the semiconductor industry is comparable to that of a big city, and any contamination in the water that can cause product defect or impact process efficiency must be removed before using. That's why UPW, water that has been treated to the highest level of purity, is extensively applied in the semiconductor industry as a cleaning and etching agent.*

3.4 Global Competition in Microchips

Ever since the advent of the Information Age, the IC-centered electronic information industry has surpassed traditional ones represented by automobile and steel manufacturing, gasoline extraction and oil by-products processing to become the largest economy sector in the world, igniting a powerful engine for world economic growth.

The IC fabrication industry demonstrated a robust growth momentum during the last 30 years. 1994 saw the first time that global IC sales volume exceeded the 100-billion threshold, reaching a total of US$109.7 billion. The number increased one-fold by the year 2000, amounting to US$200 billion. It increased again by the year 2017 arriving at US$419.7 billion, with a 22% year-on-year increase rate.

Those numbers alone could justify the accolades given to IC, lauded as the nourishment for the information industry and a multiplier force for industry development. More than that, IC fabrication technique and capacity determine to a large extent the standard and competitiveness of a country's industrial and agricultural modernization, national defense power and the position of its consumer electronic commodities, none of which could flourish without the support of a competitive international IC standing.

An increasing demand for ICs and a growing investment in it, fueled by the desire to break through its scaling limits, serve as a great driving force for the modern economy to forge ahead. Every share of IC output value can be expected to generate 10 shares of electronic devices production value and 100 shares of national economy growth value. The IC industry is a source of growth contributing more to world economy than most of other economic sectors.

Microchips have a wide range of downstream applications, including telecommunication, computers, consumer electronics, automobile, industrial and medical fields, as well as government and military fields. The following pie-chart from IC Insights shows the respective percentage of these applications in 2016, among which telecommunication and computers take up the lion's part of the total IC market share with a proportion of 74%.

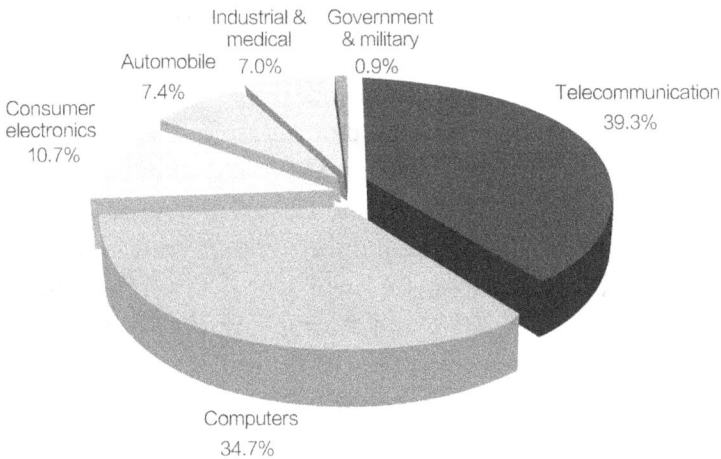

The percentage of downstream IC applications in 2016.

The remarkable growth effect brought about by the upstream IC industry to the global economy in various aspects has in turn pushed companies to intensify their search for further advancement in IC technology. While the electronics industry has been enjoying a growth rate two times of the Gross National Product value in the last few decades, IC output has actually maintained twice the growth rate of the electronics industry.

Moore's Law has for several decades guided the IC industry in setting targets for research and development and in mapping out its long-term planning. From 1975 to around 2012 in intervals of approximately 18 months, the number of components integrated onto a microchip doubled and the microchip's property and performance increased two-fold, while the cost of IC fabrication reduced by half. All of these advancements in digital electronics were consistent with and predicted by Moore's Law. This development trend in return necessitated an increasingly complex IC design and an even more demanding fabrication technique, which explained a common 20% or even 30% of investment-sales ratio in world-leading semiconductor companies like Intel and Qualcomm. For industry newcomers or followers, adequate investment is even more critical in order to catch up, considering that the installation of an advanced microchip fabrication line alone could cost around US$5–10 billion.

Let's take industrial leaders Intel and TSMC as examples to look at investment scale in the semiconductor industry. The two companies' investment sum from 2010 to 2014 stood at US$41 billion and US$47 billion respectively, indicating an annual investment of US$8 billion and US$9.5 billion. These were numbers seldom seen in other industries. The table below shows the total global investment in the IC industry from 2007 to 2016, and a surprising fact is that the investment of the top 10 or so companies put altogether accounted for about 80% of the global total investment, while the top 3 took up about half of the total investment amount.

Industry followers' investment in new microchips production line could only start to generate profit after five to six years, as it could take two to three years to install the fabrication line and to start producing commercially, and another two to three years for the output value to finally balance the manufacturing costs so as to start making a profit. It would be the same pattern with investment in IC equipment. With all the development and testing processes, it would take at least five years for investments in IC equipment to yield returns.

With increasingly demanding techniques required to produce smaller and denser microchips, investment would need to go up and returns would need a longer time to materialize. It was estimated that

Ranking of investment by world leading semiconductor companies.

Rank	2007	2008	2009	2010	2011	2012	2013	2014	2015	2016
1	Samsung	Samsung	Intel	Samsung	Intel	Samsung	Samsung	Samsung	Samsung	Samsung
2	Hynix	Intel	Samsung	TSMC	Samsung	Intel	Intel	Intel	TSMC	TSMC
3	Intel	Hynix	TSMC	Intel	TSMC	TSMC	TSMC	TSMC	Intel	Intel
4	Micron	Micron	—	Hynix	GF	SK Hynix	SK Hynix	GF	SK Hynix	Micron
5	Toshiba	Toshiba	—	GF	Micron	GF	GF	SK Hynix	Micron	SK Hynix
6	Powerchip	TSMC	—	Micron	Hynix	Micron	Micron	Micron	GF	UMC
7	TSMC	SanDisk	—	UMC	Toshiba	UMC	Toshiba	Toshiba	Sony	SMIC
8	Nanya	Infineon	—	Toshiba	UMC	Toshiba	UMC	UMC	UMC	Toshiba
9	Eipida	—	—	Nanya	Sony	Sony	—	SanDisk	Toshiba	SanDisk
10	SanDisk	—	—	TI	Infineon	ASE	—	—	Inotera	GF
11	Infineon	—	—	Eipida	SanDisk	—	—	—	SanDisk	Sony
12	ProMOS	—	—	SanDisk	ST	—	—	—	SMIC	—
13	AMD	—	—	ST	Eipida	—	—	—	—	—
14	ST	—	—	—	—	—	—	—	—	—
15	Spansion	—	—	—	—	—	—	—	—	—
16	Fujitsu	—	—	—	—	—	—	—	—	—
Total investment of the companies on the list (US$ billion)	453	241	107	399	530	450	420	506	530	533
% of the world's total investment	74%	56%	41%	74%	75%	76%	76%	77%	81%	82%

the development of the 28 nanometer technique cost US$100 million and the breakeven point for that investment was when 70 million chips were sold. The development investments for the 14 nanometer and 7 nanometer techniques were certainly much higher and had broken even only after a larger amount of chips were sold.

A huge ongoing investment, a long-term return cycle, a strict and high technology threshold and a fast and constant upgrading in relevant technologies have earned the IC industry the nickname of a money burner. However, if investments at the earlier stages worked out, the guaranteed high profit rate of this industry will turn all the investments into a money churning machine called IC technology and patents. (Read on for a write-up about Qualcomm that shows how lucrative IC technology and patents can be.)

From the above table, it is easy to see that the top players in the global semiconductor industry put in the highest investment and take up the biggest market share. They seem to have an unshakable advantage in the full suite of procedures in IC manufacturing, including designing, fabrication, equipment and packaging. Industrial giants like Intel, Samsung, TSMC and Qualcomm dominate the whole market with their technology and patents, which bring them a steady flow of money.

In contrast, those companies who are outside the MVPs club would find it difficult and almost impossible to compete in the world market due to barriers caused by investment, technologies and talents, and many of them could face great uncertainties. Others in the middle of the pyramid structure draw lessons from the industrial leaders' success experience to rise up quickly through mergers and acquisitions.

The IC industry is also characterized by a high concentration of qualified electronics engineers who play the role of inventing and steering the technology. As far as technology is concerned, we have spent quite a few pages to elaborate on the strategic significance of mastering core technologies in the semiconductor industry. However, sharing or exchange of technology is also a driving force in the advancement of semiconductors.

Qualcomm's Royalty Business: Highly Lucrative yet Controversial

The entire chapter 2 is about the importance of core technologies in the semiconductor industry. There is a saying that goes like this: third raters profit on labor, second raters profit on products, first raters profit on technology and the most capable of all profit on patents. How valuable are patents and what economic return can they bring? In Qualcomm's case, the money earned from its patent licensing businesses has played a critical role in propelling it to become a dominant force in the global semiconductor industry. Chinese companies have dubbed Qualcomm's somewhat convoluted and incredibly lucrative patent royalty scheme as Qualcomm tax, which is paid to the mobile chip maker for using its patented wireless technology for every smartphone produced in China and other countries too.

Most people may think of Qualcomm as a chip-making enterprise since the company's Snapdragon line of chips is in almost every major flagship smartphone. However, the chip maker also has thousands of patents that underlie basic wireless network standards adopted by mobile carriers, telecoms equipment makers and smartphone manufacturers. The bulk of its profit comes from patents it owns that give basic cellular connectivity to smartphones. In the year 2016 alone, the company's royalty licensing division reported US$6.5 billion of pretax profit on US$7.6 billion of revenue. Meanwhile, its chip business only made US$1.8 billion in pretax profit on US$15.4 billion of sales.

Qualcomm's practice of charging patent royalties is based on the device's total value, as opposed to just the value of the mobile chips inside the device. ARM charges a 1–2% patent licensing fee according to the price of a particular component directly from components makers instead of engaging smartphone makers. Qualcomm, on the contrary, forces smartphone makers to pay a 4–6% royalty for every product based on the device's total price. For every iPhone sold at US$649, Apple pays about US$15 to Qualcomm. For the higher-end US$749 iPhone it pays slightly more, and even more for the US$849 iPhone.

Many people have condemned Qualcomm's device-based royalties. They said that it has in fact constituted discrimination which is prohibited by fair trade regulations, because the makers of high-end smartphones are paying far more for access to the same patented technology than the makers of cheaper devices.

The legal battles against Qualcomm started when China cracked down on the chipmaker's alleged practice of overcharging and abusing dominance in the Chinese market in 2015. China imposed a US$975 million fine and new deals to lower patent licensing fees for Chinese customers. Following that, the European Commission opened antitrust investigations against the US company; and then the Korea Fair Trade Commission slapped a nearly US$1 billion fine on Qualcomm. Apple and other large smartphone makers like Samsung appeared to see an opportunity to challenge Qualcomm's highly profitable but controversial licensing model.

This model has been referred to as a virtual cycle, which means that Qualcomm's two business divisions of chip-making and patent-licensing sustain each other in that the former creates patents and the latter fuels R&D for more chips. A change to this arrangement is imperative as Qualcomm is besieged by the world's main economic entities and smartphone makers, but the ultimate goal would be to keep its golden goose — the patent licensing business — intact.

1. *Microchip's New Frontier*

In an era when Moore's Law no longer applies, when it is getting ever more challenging to fabricate smaller microelectronic components, will the IC technology reach its limit and end with the 7 nanometer or 3 nanometer technique as predicted by many?

We have broken one limit after another with regards to semiconductor technology. It was believed in the 1970s that 1 micrometer was the limit of how small IC components could be. When that limit was torn down, 0.1 micrometer became the new limit in the 1980s and then 0.05 micrometer in the 1990s.

Who would have thought that one day, humans would be capable of maneuvering upon 7 nanometer components on the surface of a silicon wafer? Now, the International Technology Roadmap for Semiconductors (ITRS) has predicted that it is possible to achieve the last and final generation of the Complementary Metal-Oxide Semiconductor (CMOS) transistor, but the gate electrode pattern in

IC fabrication bears no hope of scaling down under 3 nanometer unless scientists break through the limitation of physics in the macro world.

The semiconductor industry has always been devoted to the search for new breakthroughs through inter-industrial and inter-disciplinary integration with mechanics, optics and biology. New technologies and industries have emerged, among which optoelectronic integrated devices, quantum microchips and biology microchips are the new frontiers for microchips.

(1) Optoelectronic Microchips

In 2015, researchers at Massachusetts Institute of Technology (MIT) successfully produced a working optoelectronic chip that operated electronically like all the other microchips but used light to transfer electronic information. The chip integrated 850 optical components and 70 million transistors. Although it was outshone by the billion-odd transistors in a typical microprocessor, the chip demonstrated all the functionalities that a commercial microchip would require.

The Photonic Devices and Photonic Integration Research Center of the Xi'an Institute of Optics and Precision Mechanics under the CAS has been pioneering China's photonic integrated circuits development. Cheng Dong, its director, predicted that the optoelectronic microchips market will grow at an exciting 38% annual rate and is expected to reach a global sales volume of US$30 billion in 2025 while generating a US$10 trillion market for cloud computing, 5G application, AI, internet of things (IoT) and live streaming video.

(2) Quantum Microchips

The development of quantum microchips which integrate quantum logic gates and quantum bits is a crucial step for the creation of the quantum computer. By taking shortcuts through many calculations, it could effectively simulate things that are difficult for today's computers to do. IBM developed such a superconducting chip after stumbling through several errors in 2015. Other internet giants including Google and Microsoft have since been investing into the research on quantum computer, which will hopefully be the next milestone in the Information Age. In February 2018, China's quantum microchip project led by Professor Guo Guoping of the University of Science and Technology of China unveiled the working mechanics of the three-qubits (quantum bit) logic gate, which is a stepping stone toward the realization of quantum computation.

(3) Biology Microchips

Biological microchips integrate biological systems with microchips. For example, it isolates and harnesses a biological process in which energy is produced through ion pumps powered by ATP, the biological world's energy currency molecule, to power integrated circuit. By doing so, ion pumps actually act similarly to transistors. An artificially created biological component with IC will greatly extend the range of possibilities in electronics. As Columbia engineering professor Ken Shepard said, "100 Intel designers couldn't design a system that could tell if there is a skunk in the room or not, and the best synthetic biologists in the world couldn't build a radio. If we can just use the piece of the biological process that we want and use its function with solid state electronics, we will get that enhanced functional palette of capacities that don't exist with either of them alone."

References

1. Peter Van Zant. *Microchips Fabrication: A Practical Guide to Semiconductor Processing*. McGraw-Hill Education. 2014.
2. Lu Jing. *The Practical Technology in Integrated Circuit Manufacturing* [M]. Beijing: China Machine Press. 2011.
3. Kikuchi Masanori. *Into the Heart of Our Hi-tech Era: The World of Semiconductors* [M]. Science Press. 2012.
4. Zou Shichang, Hai Bo, Qin Chang. *The World of Microchips: Into Integrated Circuits* [M]. East China Normal University Press. 2017.
5. Liu Yan. *50 Years of Integrated Circuits*. SinoTech. 2008.

6. Gan Xuewen. *The Mechanism and Designing of Integrated Circuits.* Peking University Press. 2006.

7. *The History of Microchips.* Institute of Computer Technology of China Academy of Science. 2018.

Chapter 4

Stars on the Stage of Microchips

Overture

Santa Clara Valley, later known as Silicon Valley for its fame in leading the world's silicon industry, is a 48-kilometer-long and 16-kilometer-wide area. Here lies America's most advanced electronics industrial center, gathering about 96% of the country's semiconductor companies.

It is a hotbed of new electronics technology and a breeding ground for entrepreneurship. Fairchild, a true pioneer and the West Point of semiconductors, grew and thrived in this place, like a full-bloom dandelion whose seeds went far and wide with the power of the wind.

While we witness stars and superstars on the competitive and brutal stage of semiconductors, we also observe smaller players fleeting by and then disappearing into the unknown.

History has witnessed many dark hours on the stage.

The light, however, never fails to brighten the way ahead.

The people who are crazy enough to think that they can change the world are the ones who do.
                                    — Steve Jobs, Co-founder of Apple

4.1 The Greatest Invention After Wheels

America, a secluded land far away from the battlefields and destruction of World War I and World War II, attracted large inflows of top talents.

It was able to provide them with abundant resources and an integrated industrial layout for scientific research and products incubation. From the 1940s onwards, America has been at the forefront of global technology advancement and high-end industry development with its series of epoch-making inventions and creations.

Microchip is one of the revolutionary and transformative inventions of the time.

A core component for almost all electronic devices that's worth thousands of billions of dollars in the global market and a significant deterrence weapon used in global power games, microchips actually stemmed from an experimental observation in AT&T's Bell Labs. It was found that when two gold point contacts were applied to a crystal of germanium, a signal was produced with the output power greater than the input.

Solid-state physics group leader William Shockley saw the potential in the observation and worked many months to expand the knowledge of semiconductors. He decided to present this new finding to his colleagues before the Christmas holiday started. On 23rd December 1947, Shockley showed up at the Bell Labs office in the early morning and was shortly joined by John Bardeen and Walter Brattain to check the display experiment to be presented in the afternoon. The experiment was to show the prospect of replacing vacuum tubes with a smaller, lighter, faster and more efficient point-contact amplifier.

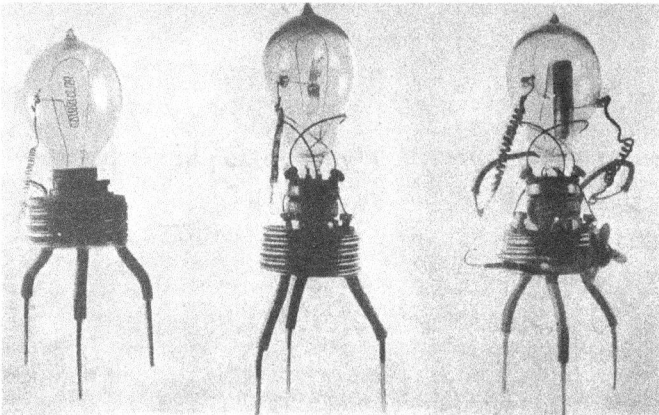

Earlier-stage transistors.

The gold point contact experiment, completed during a distant telephony process which involved the cooperation of oscilloscope, signal generator, transformer, microphone, earphone, ammeter and alteration switch, was witnessed by dozens of researchers from Bell Labs. They were amazed to see the sharp surge in the oscillograph which indicated a significant amplification of the signal input.

When they heard the voice of Brattain being transmitted by the signal, it was proof that this new device actually worked. This group of the world's best scientists became excited because they sensed what they saw that day was going to change the world.

(From left) Bardeen, Shockley and Brattain in Bell Labs in 1948.

This world-changing device was later called the transistor, a term coined as a contraction of transresistance. Compared with large and power-consuming vacuum tubes, transistors are small in size and energy efficient, which enabled them to be manufactured in large numbers and applied in various occasions. The miniaturization of electronic devices brought by the wide application of transistors ushered in a new era of electrical and electronic engineering.

William Shockley (first person seated from the right) celebrating his 1956 Nobel Prize in Physics with his colleagues.

1. *The Birth of Integrated Circuits*

The invention and the commercial application of transistors made the birth of integrated circuits a decade later a natural course and also a necessity. Actually, as early as in the 1930s, there were engineers and scientists who had already conceived the idea of an integrated circuit which involved the arrangement of electronic components onto a substrate to form a functional circuit unit. They had also published papers about it or patented the idea. However, their attempts to build such a circuitry were unsuccessful.

Then, Jack Kilby came up with a new and revolutionary design in which the assembling of circuit components on a single piece of semiconductor material would deliver the functionality of an entire electronic module. Later, Robert Noyce's silicon version of the design and the associated fabrication techniques made integrated circuits truly practical in the manufacturing industry. Kilby and Noyce were credited as the co-inventors of integrated circuits.

In 1947 when the transistor was first invented, Kilby received his bachelor of science degree in electrical engineering from the University of Illinois. Three years later in 1950 when he was working at Centrallab, he earned his master's degree from the University of Wisconsin. The rapid advancement of electronics technology ignited in the young man's heart an ardent passion to devote himself to the progress of this revolutionary technological transformation.

In 1958, 34-year-old Kilby was employed by Texas Instruments to work on the miniaturization of circuitry components, which was then commonly referred to as the problem of "the tyranny of numbers". In the middle of 1958, he spent the summer working on the problem while his colleagues were enjoying their vacations. It turned out that being a newly employed engineer who had yet to be granted a summer vacation did Kilby some immense good, because he made full use of his time to examine in depth previous circuitry designs and finally came to his own conclusion that could provide a solution for the problem. He theorized that germanium could be used to make all common electronic components like resistors and capacitors, and he could build a single-slab circuitry integrated with all components that could combine the functionality of the entire electronic module.

Jack Kilby.

On 12th September, after Texas Instruments employees came back from their vacation, Kilby presented his findings to the company's management. A piece of germanium the size about four square millimeters on which 20-odd components had been integrated, an oscilloscope attached to the germanium and a switch constituted Kilby's presentation. As he pressed the switch, the oscilloscope showed a continuous sine wave, indicating that his circuitry was successful in functioning as a complete unit.

That day was officially recognized as the birthday of integrated circuits. On 6th February 1959, Kilby filed a patent application to the US Patent Office for "miniaturized electronic circuits", and the patent that announced the invention of integrated circuits was coded 3138743.

On the west coast, Noyce led the "traitorous eight" to leave Shockley Laboratory and co-founded Fairchild Semiconductor Corporation in San Jose, California. Nearly at the same time as Kilby succeeded in miniaturizing circuitry, Noyce brought up his own idea about making integrated circuits truly practical in manufacturing. Half a year after Kilby's presentation at Texas Instruments, Noyce independently developed a new variety of silicon-based integrated circuit. It was more practical than Kilby's implementation and enabled large-scale commercial manufacture. In July 1959, Noyce filed a patent on semiconductor device-and-lead structure, which later became a fundamental technique in IC fabrication.

In the same year, Jean Hoerni, a member of the traitorous eight, developed the groundbreaking planar process for reliably fabricating semiconductor devices such as transistors on IC substrate. These two IC manufacturing techniques developed in Fairchild Semiconductor, together with many others, combined to form a powerful engine that boosted the development of the company in the following years.

Fairchild was a pioneer in the manufacturing of transistors and integrated circuits. The first batch of semiconductor industry leaders and engineers were once employees of the company. After leaving Fairchild, they started their own enterprises and left their own footprints in the industry. A legendary example is Intel, founded by Noyce and Gordon Moore, which became the next shining star of the semiconductor industry.

To many Chinese, Noyce was a superstar in the same stratosphere of the legendary Silicon Valley. He embodied the perfect combination of talent, wealth and achievements, and of scientist, entrepreneur and adventurer.

Robert Noyce in Fairchild Semiconductors.

When Noyce was asked how he managed to invent integrated circuits during his 1984 visit to China, he replied quickly that it was all thanks to his laziness which drove him to search for an easier and simpler way of integrating electronic components on the semiconductor substrate instead of using wires.

2. *A Co-invention that Re-shaped the World*

Kilby and Noyce received the Franklin Institute's Stuart Ballantine Medal in 1966, the former for "inventing the first integrated circuit" and the latter for "bringing up the theory for mass manufacturing of integrated circuit". Three years later, the US Federal Court legally credited the invention of integrated circuits to both Kilby and Noyce, and the patents filed by Texas Instruments and Fairchild Semiconductors were acknowledged as the proof to patent certain aspects of integrated circuits.

In the same year, the two companies struck a deal which admitted each other's patent rights on IC and ordered that any IC manufacturers should be obliged to obtain relevant patent-using warranty from both of them. This patent licensing scheme established since the 1960s fetched loads of money for the two companies.

In 2000, 10 years after the death of Noyce, Kilby was awarded the Nobel Prize in Physics for his breakthrough invention of the first integrated circuit. He shared his personal thoughts on the semiconductor industry and its history in his acceptance speech. Then US President Bill Clinton congratulated him by writing, "You can take pride in the knowledge that your work will help to improve lives for generations to come". It was a pity that Noyce was not around to share this award. However, he was remembered by many for his incredible contributions. Different from Kilby who spent all his life devoted to semiconductor research in Texas Instruments, Noyce was a successful scientist as well as a visionary and sharp entrepreneur, evident in the two companies he co-founded, Fairchild and Intel.

IC's mass production capability, reliability, miniaturization and building-block position in virtually all electronic equipment have revolutionized the world of electronics where computers, mobile phones and other digital home appliances are now inextricable parts of the structure of modern societies. It is an invention as world-changing and revolutionary as wheels, and it has been lending itself to a whole new series of inventions that would certainly add to the advancement of human society.

In 1999, the *Los Angeles Times* published a list of the 20th century's 50 most economically influential people. Shockley together with Kilby and Noyce were elected as number one on the list, followed by such prominent names as Henry Ford, the captain of the automobile industry and a business magnate; Franklin Roosevelt, one of the greatest US presidents along with George Washington and Abraham Lincoln; and Walt Disney, the US cultural icon who held the record for the most number of Academy Awards earned by an individual.

When Kilby died in 2005 at age 81 after a brief battle with cancer in his home in Dallas, Texas, integrated circuits had grown from a piece of simple-structured circuitry on his laboratory desk to a global industry with an annual sales volume of US$190 billion and a peripheral electronic devices market totaling US$1,275 billion. Since then till now and into the future, the IC industry has been and will be growing at a continuously thrilling rate.

Tom Engibous, the Texas Instruments Director, President and CEO, remarked in his eulogy for Kilby, "It's true that Jack's invention of the integrated circuit touches all of our lives dozens of times every day, in ways that range from the mundane to the miraculous… Changing the world is exactly what Jack did, in ways that are still unfolding. Thanks to his invention, our world is on the cusp of artificial eyes that will let blind people see… prosthetic devices that amputees can control with their minds… and even cars that safely drive themselves."

4.2 Fairchild, the One that Gives Silicon Valley its Name

Shockley, Noyce, and the traitorous eight were all inextricably linked to a company's name, one that incubated Silicon Valley and pioneered the early history of semiconductor — Fairchild.

It all started in 1955 when Shockley left Bell Labs to work on silicon-based semiconductor devices and opened the Shockley Semiconductor Laboratory one year later in Mountain View, California with an aim of mass-producing transistors.

It was said that Shockley initially tried to hire some of his former workers from Bell Labs but none of them wanted to leave the east coast, which was then the center for the most advanced hi-tech research. Then he succeeded in recruiting a group of eight young PhD graduates and gave them the goal of developing and producing new semiconductor devices.

These eight were real geniuses, all under 30, all in the prime of their creativity and imagination. Jean Hoerni (1924–1997), a Switzerland-born dual-PhD in physics who worked at the California Institute of

Technology; Victor Grinich, a Stanford University PhD who was a researcher at SRI (Stanford Research Institute) International; Eugene Kleiner, who worked in Western Electric, the manufacturing arm of AT&T Corporation; Gordon Moore, a postdoctoral researcher at the Applied Physics Laboratory at Johns Hopkins University; Robert Noyce, a MIT PhD and a research engineer at the Philco Corporation in Philadelphia; and Julius Blank, Jay Last, and Sheldon Roberts. All of them gathered under Shockley's attempt to commercialize a new transistor design. They were prepared to blaze the trail and revolutionize the electronics industry, but in a rather unexpected way, as it turned out later.

Fairchild eight, dubbed by Shockley as the traitorous eight, gathered before the emblem of Fairchild.

They were slightly taken aback at their first sight of the Shockley Laboratory, as it was devoid of research equipment and it reeked of pungent new paint. It could barely be called a laboratory, not yet at least. Worst of all, Shockley was far from an easy-going and friendly boss, unreasonable even, despite being known for his genius charisma radiating out from his seminars and speeches, and his big reputation as a Nobel Prize winner. His management of the group was authoritarian and unpopular, as "he had no idea how to manage and he was a disastrously bad businessman".

Shockley's paranoid, micromanaging personality was accentuated by the fact that his research focus was not proving fruitful. Moore later revealed that Shockley's initial business ambition was to manufacture commercial transistors sold at US$0.05 each, a price not realized even 25 years later in 1980. After this failure to commercialize transistors, Shockley completely shifted his efforts from the research on diffusion bipolar transistors to the development of Shockley diodes, despite the strong disagreement of his members, which later was proven to be a strategic mistake.

This focus on fine-tuning Shockley diodes for mass production reduced the transistor production devices to commercial failures, and kept the company from producing any viable commercial products. The Shockley team started losing its members and the eight key employees made up their decisions too.

They wanted to work on their own project, starting with plans to make silicon transistors, at a time when germanium was still the most common material for semiconductor use. They needed an investor who could be convinced to the future they envisioned. In August 1957, they received Sherman Fairchild of Fairchild Camera and Instrument, an eastern US company with considerable military contracts. Fairchild was impressed by Noyce's impassioned presentation of his idea of using silicon as substrate and of his vision that silicon semiconductors would herald a time of cheap electronic components and disposable appliances. Within several weeks, the Fairchild Semiconductor division was established with a loan of US$1.38 million provided by the Fairchild parent company.

In September, the eight key members of the Shockley Labs — Blank, Grinich, Hoerni, Kleiner, Last, Moore, Noyce, and Roberts resigned and left. They became known as the "traitorous eight" in the good sense, and established themselves as the core of Fairchild, the undisputable semiconductor leader at the time. They became Silicon Valley legends, who pioneered, created and inspired in the next decades to come.

Once they got started, they became fully immersed in a single goal to produce their first product, a double diffused silicon mesa transistor. They were all very young (aged between 27–32), only a few years beyond their school days and mostly starting their families and raising young children, yet they devoted all their time and effort to building Fairchild. It was a likeminded, innovative, hardworking and entrepreneurial group. In November 1957, the eight men moved out of Grinich's garage into a new empty building on the border of Palo Alto. They immediately set a clear goal of developing an array of silicon diffusion mesa transistors for application in digital devices.

Necessity is sometimes the best incentive for innovation. The eight young men were pushed along in their cause by the momentous period in which they lived. One well-known event that occurred at the time was the Soviet Union taking the lead in the Space Race by successfully sending its astronauts into space, and the US was pulling out all the stops to make a remarkable comeback. The government-level necessity for miniaturized electronic components and devices brought a great opportunity for Fairchild. In January 1958, Fairchild received its first order from IBM, which demanded 100 silicon transistors for its computer storage system. In July–September of the same year, Fairchild developed a new technology that resulted in a higher yield of operational transistors. By the end of the year, the company, started by the traitorous eight and predicted by Shockley as "would achieve nothing", already had a revenue of US$500,000 and more than 100 employees, making itself a rising star in Silicon Valley.

Before long, Fairchild transistors were considered for the Minuteman I Guidance Computer, but they did not meet military standards of reliability. Fairchild actually had a solution for that in the planar technology developed by Hoerni, which unfortunately went unnoticed after it was first proposed. In the following weeks, the eight men spent nights after nights on experiments with the first planar transistors and the technology turned out to be the second most important event in the history of microelectronics after the invention of transistors.

Planar technology, the prototype for today's IC lithography process, was used to fabricate individual components of a transistor and connect transistors together in an easier way, at a lower cost and with higher performance and reliability. The series of mechanism (rather similar to the mechanism of modern photolithography but more focused on the fabrication of transistors) involved the use of photographic processing to mask a layer of light exposed chemicals onto the two-dimensional projection transformed from a circuit pattern, and the use of a series of exposures on a silicon substrate to create insulators and conductors.

Planar process enabled researchers at Fairchild to create circuits on the surface of a silicon crystal slice by creating and connecting transistors without the need of manually wiring them together, which not only greatly speeded up the mass production process but also remarkably enhanced the property of the transistors so as to meet the military standard of reliability. With this new technology, Fairchild immediately held the leadership in the manufacturing of transistors.

Hoerni's innovation of the planar technique did a great favor not only to the fabrication of transistors but also to the building of integrated circuits. After Kilby presented the first working IC in the laboratory of Texas Instruments in September 1958, Noyce brought about the practical manufacturing technique using the planar process and made the mass production of ICs commercially possible.

The successful commercialization of IC and Fairchild's patent rights on the associated technologies gave it an annual revenue of US$90 million, and the company grew from 12 to more than 12,000 employees. The 1960s witnessed Fairchild's golden age, with a doubling of revenue every year from 1960 to 1965, reaching US$200 million in 1997. By the year 1966, it had become the world's second largest semiconductor company, ranking behind only Texas Instruments.

Notably, in 1965, Moore published a paper describing a doubling trend every other year in the number of components per integrated circuit, which was known as Moore's Law. The Law was later revised by himself to "double every 18 months" and had been proven true by the industry development route. For the next half century, it was guiding the research target and long-term planning of the semiconductor industry.

Just when Fairchild Semiconductor was churning out new products and raking in money, an inner split began to creep in. It started with the disagreement on profit distribution between the founders and the parent company, which led to the job-hopping of four of the traitorous eight. Only Blank, Grinich, Moore and Noyce stayed back in 1961. The conflict failed to be resolved and caused a rift between the founders of Fairchild and new incoming engineers. Both the core employees who chose to stay back and the new ones who joined later started to ponder their future paths. Many set out to start their own ventures instead of clinging to a mothership who tended to neglect and was reluctant to share profit. Among them, the most well-known ones include:

- Bob Widler, who accepted an offer to join National Semiconductor's Molectro facility in Santa Clara at the end of 1965.
- Charles Sporck, who in March 1967 was hired by National Semiconductor as chief executive officer and president and brought with him four other Fairchild personnel.
- Robert Noyce left Fairchild together with Gordon Moore and founded the semiconductor company Intel in July 1968.
- Jerry Sanders, along with seven other employees from Fairchild, left to found Advanced Micro Devices (AMD) in May 1969.

This exodus of Fairchild employees to set up new companies in the Bay Area helped shape the way Silicon Valley came into being and the way it innovated, influenced and led. Fairchild was so entrenched in the creation of new corporations in Santa Clara and the output of experienced electronics engineers that in a semiconductor engineering conference held in 1969, only 24 of the 400 attendants had not worked in Fairchild.

"Silicon Valley" was first used in a public report when Don Hoefler, a journalist who was writing for *Electronic News*, named his series of articles that started from 11th January 1971 about the history of the semiconductor industry in the Bay Area as "Silicon Valley USA". The series is the first "behind-the-scenes report of the men, money, and litigation which spawned 23 companies, from the fledgling rebels of Shockley Transistor to the present day (1971)". Later, Everett Rogers who wrote *Silicon Valley Fever*, a bestseller in the early 1980s, said that

Fairchild was directly or indirectly involved in the creation of dozens of semiconductor corporations and that a Fairchild working experience could knock the door open to nearly every other peer companies at the time.

Fairchild is a legend in Silicon Valley history not only because it pioneered the manufacturing and innovation of transistors and integrated circuits, or it nurtured a group of scientists, engineers and entrepreneurs who grew to be prominent persons in the field, or it ushered in an era of exponential advancement in the global semiconductor industry (China was being plagued by its own troubles at this time, which shall be touched on in the next chapter), but also because it still shines brightly in the areas of innovation and aspiration even till today.

4.3 Intel, the One that Leads by Innovation

Intel, a name combines the words *integrated* and *electronics*, has become synonymous with intelligence information during the course of its 50 years. It is the world's second largest and second highest-valued semiconductor chip manufacturer. Bill Gates views it as the king of microchips and one of the world's most invaluable enterprises.

Although we cannot predict the future of this semiconductor giant, we can look into its history and find inspiration and helpful lessons there.

Intel was founded by Noyce and Moore in 1968 in Mountain View, California, with an investment of US$2.5 million after they left Fairchild. The new company was initially distinguished by its ability to make logic circuits using semiconductor devices. Its first product, the small, high-speed memory chips 3101 and 3301 made a quick and welcomed entry into the market, and immediately phased out the old magnetic-core memory chip.

Intel's business grew during the 1970s as it expanded and improved its manufacturing processes and produced a wider range of products dominated by various memory devices. With the commercial success of 3101 and 3301, Intel did not fail to see their flaws and swiftly developed DRAM, a faster and cheaper mainframe memory device which quickly became the industry standard of the time. From the outset, Intel was always focused on improving the property and performance of its microchip products to keep pace with and even lead the needs of electronic device makers. The founders knew their only way to stand out in the changeable environment of hi-tech business competition was to invest generously into product improvement and innovation.

Intel's first 100 employees in front of its Mountain View headquarters in 1969.

For that purpose, Intel put in extra work to formulate a mechanism to smooth out the undesirable out-sync and bottleneck between its R&D center and its manufacturing department so as to make sure that there was a direct express line for the transformation of its new technologies in the laboratory up into its production workshop and then out into the market. By the end of the 1970s, Intel was showing an absolute dominance in the memory microchip market with a nearly 90% market share.

In 1983, on the eve of its business focus shift amidst Japanese manufacturers' fierce competition in the memory market, Intel's annual sales volume reached US$1 billion for the first time. Its robust economic performance continued even in the turbulent 2001 when the US internet economic bubble burst and the Nasdaq index plummeted, closing with an annual revenue of US$26.5 billion. In 2017, this prominent leader in the semiconductor industry announced a revenue of US$62.8 billion and a gross profit of US$9.6 billion, soaring to a stock value of US$236.5 billion.

Intel's impressive market performance could not be achieved without the series of innovations and new products launched during the course of its history:

- In 1969, Intel launched the world's first bipolar 64-bit Static Random-Access Memory (SRAM) named 3101, and memory chips became its major revenue contributor until the early 1980s.
- In 1971, Intel created the first commercially available microprocessor (Intel 4004).
- In 1972, Intel designed and manufactured the first 8-bit microprocessor (Intel 8008).
- In 1978, Intel developed the first 16-bit microprocessor (Intel 8086) which gave rise to the later x86 architecture.
- In 1982, Intel introduced its 8086-based microprocessor (Intel 286) which was also 16-bit and used approximately 134,000 transistors.
- In 1985, Intel launched a 32-bit microprocessor (Intel 386), which used about 275,000 transistors and were used as the CPU of many workstations and high-end personal computers of the time.

- In 1989, Intel designed the 486 microprocessor (Intel 486), a higher-performance follow-up of the previous Intel 386, which was the first x86 chip to use more than a million transistors.
- In 1993, Intel introduced its P5 microprocessor, the first of its Pentium series of x86 architecture-compatible microprocessors, which used approximately 300 million transistors.

Since the release of Intel's first P5 microprocessor in 1993, a follow-up series of its improved Pentium products started and fueled an upgrading wave and a price revolution in electronic devices. Today, every 8 out of 10 personal computers in the world are installed with Intel's microprocessors. They, together with other electronic devices deployed in households, factories, governments and even the space, are transforming our lives for all and for good.

After scooping its first barrel of gold from memory business, Intel's range of principal products now sprawls across systems and devices, processors, boards and kits, chipsets, programmable devices, memory and storage, server products, software and services, and technologies. To take the lead in the ever-growing electronics industry for 5 years might not be difficult, but to do it for more than half a century certainly entails some extraordinary effort and vision, because there would always be challenges that need to be tended to. In the mid-1980s, Intel underwent the worst recession in its history, but the company would emerge from it transformed.

In the 1980s, the electronics market had been in boom and bust for years, semiconductor component products were becoming undifferentiated and Japanese companies were flooding the memory market with underpriced chips which were subsidized by the Japanese government. Over the course of the final eight months of 1985, Intel saw the price of a memory product fall from US$17 to US$4.50. It was a miserable year for Intel and the rest of the electronics industry in America. The company lost money for the first time since it had gone public in 1971.

When the recession hit, Intel was both a microprocessor and memory company. While the former business was thriving, the latter was becoming nearly impossible to maintain.

Before we delve into how Intel made it through the difficult times, we shall first detail its rise in the personal computer CPU market. Before the 1980s, IBM dominated the mainframe computer devices and the computing platform market with its self-developed mainframe System 360 and 370 and the operating systems that ran on them. Intel, in contrast, was confined the lower-end and less-demanding processor market sectors because its microprocessors were underperforming compared with IBM's mainframe system.

Mainframe systems were used to make mainframe computers which were then accessible and affordable to a limited number of big institutions and corporations. The market for minicomputers, later called personal computers, had not emerged yet and probably was not expected to emerge at all, although the invention of integrated circuits did remarkably and economically scale down the size of computing machines. Thomas Watson, the Chairman and CEO of IBM from 1914 to 1956, was believed to have said a well-known and now-ironical statement in 1943, "I think there is a world market for maybe 5 computers". Now, there is a world market for computers of maybe twice the number of the global population.

With the availability and popularization of personal computers in the latter half of the 1970s, Intel's microprocessors finally found their potential. In 1974, Intel designed and launched its second 8-bit microprocessor 8080 which directly influenced the ubiquitous 32-bit and 64-bit architecture of today. In 1976, the Apple Computer Company (now Apple) released its first product, Apple I, a desktop computer designed and hand-built by Steve Wozniak. One year later, the Apple II, an 8-bit home computer the size of a common television plus a typewriter which defined the appearance of today's computers, was successfully mass-produced and referred to by the press as the "1977 Trinity". The original retail price for Apple II was US$1,298 (equivalent to US$5,364 in 2018), a price affordable by many small enterprises. Industry analysts estimated a market of 250,000 minicomputers among small-to-medium enterprises in America.

The initially lower-end and less-demanding market sectors started to boom with an exponential growth rate, and the electronics revolution ignited by the rising demand of personal computers was gaining momentum. Not only start-ups like Apple and Compaq were stirring up new ideas and bringing out new designs, but old companies like IBM and HP also began to march into the personal computer market to get their fingers in the pie. In 1980, the Big Blue (IBM) released its very first personal computer, a move that was described by the press as "a giant entered the world of Lilliput".

Intel's specialization and experience in microprocessor development and manufacturing fitted well with the rising personal computer market. It outdid IBM's CPU products in many aspects. Seeing that it would be unwise to compete with Intel in the CPU market, IBM exited and turned to purchasing microprocessors from Intel.

Due to a busy market for personal computers, Intel's supply of microprocessors actually fell short of the demand in 1984. They had to turn down some not-so-important customers to guarantee adequate supplies for the big ones.

Given the atmosphere of supply scarcity in 1984, Intel started a major manufacturing expansion and even licensed other semiconductor manufacturers to produce for them. The market, however, like any market at any time, could be volatile and unpredictable. The personal computer boom collapsed in the fourth quarter of 1984. The industry went into an abrupt slump just as a significant amount of new semiconductor capacity were added throughout the world. The demand projections of 1984 became instant relics in 1985, creating a capacity glut and a severe downward price spiral. Intel was left with an operation structure appropriate to the US$2–3 billion company it wanted to be rather than the US$1.0–1.5 billion company it was becoming. At the same time, in the face of aggressive targeting by Japanese competitors, Intel was obliged to defend its industry-leading market share for the erasable, programmable, read-only memories (EPROM) in which it had always been the technology and market leader. As a result, Intel's 1985 revenues were 16% lower than the previous year's record of US$1.6 billion and its net income essentially disappeared. 1986 saw the company's first loss of US$173 million since 1971.

Three strategic measures taken by Intel, among many other necessary adjustments in its operations including plant closings, layoffs, salary cuts and time off without pay, got it out of the mire. First, Intel continued its investments in research and development in order to maintain its product leadership in the face of rapid evolution of technology and short product life cycles. In 1985, Intel increased its R&D spending to US$195 million, or 14.3% of revenues to maintain all critical programs and enhance those promising ones. In 1986, Intel spent US$228 million in R&D, equal to 18% of its revenues and an increase of US$33 million over 1985.

Second, in response to the aggressive pricing in the market for components and systems products, Intel focused its efforts towards increasing productivity, not only in the factory but also in engineering and administrative chores. US$446 million (US$210 million for 1985 and US$236 million for 1986) was spent on capital equipment for automation updating to meet the requirements of new manufacturing technology.

Thirdly, Intel decided to phase out of the DRAM business in 1985 and sold its bubble memory business in 1986. The two memory components businesses had proved to become over-crowded and loss-plagued niche markets targeted by competitive Japanese companies. Intel chose to focus on the development of manufacturing technology to remain competitive in its memory products, in particular to target EPROMs as a product to drive its technology and refine its manufacturing process.

These moves were documented by many business books, especially the gut-wrenching decision to shift from DRAM to microprocessors under the guidance of Grove and Moore. They eventually steered the company to dominate the personal computer market via the x86 processor line.

Thanks to these moves and events, Intel's component and system-level product line got remarkably strengthened. The Intel 386 microprocessor released in 1985 perfectly exemplified this strength. Intel 386 was received by the market with unprecedented enthusiasm because of its compatibility with the large base of already-existing software and its architectural enhancements. Prior to 386, the difficulty of manufacturing and the instability of reliable supply meant that a mass-produced semiconductor needed to be multi-sourced under manufacturing license from the originating company. Grove made a bold decision that 386 would not be outsourced but only available from Intel itself, a decision later proved to be ultimately crucial to Intel's success in the market. IBM had the manufacturing rights for the earlier Intel 286 microprocessor so it stuck to using 286 until 1991. It was obliged to strike a new deal with Intel to acquire the manufacturing license for 386 to be used solely in its own personal computers and boards.

Intel 386 microprocessor.

To make better use of the memory management capabilities of Intel's 386 microprocessor, Microsoft developed the revolutionary Windows 3.0, which included a significantly enhanced user interface as well as technical improvements. The collaboration between Microsoft Windows and Intel processors gained ascendance and their ongoing alliance, dubbed "Wintel", continued to give them market dominance. The release and success of 386 set Intel on the track to a consecutive 11 years of record-setting revenues from 1988 onwards. 386 was the most complete and most favorably received microprocessors in Intel's history up to then. Orders flew in from micro communications, automobiles and the US Army Material Command.

In the fourth quarter of 1989, Intel began volume shipments of its newly developed 486 microprocessors. Demand for 386/486 products exceeded supply. Combining compatibility, upgrade ability and connectivity, the microprocessor family had become the de facto standard for many business computing applications, and a common computing platform for notebooks, laptops and desktop computers, servers, workstations and mainframes in both single-processor and multi-processor configurations. In 1992, Intel reaped for the first time a net profit of more than US$1 billion, and the Wintel alliance was poised to take over the leadership of IBM in the computer industry.

In 1993, Intel introduced the first of its many Pentium microprocessors, which continued to create "a seemingly unending spiral of falling prices and rising performance". As a direct extension of the previous 486 architecture, the Pentium series was a member of the software compatible x86 microprocessors family. Intel's market capitalization reached an all-time high of US$509 billion, indicating a bright public opinion of its prospects and a booming investment confidence towards its market performance.

Intel emerged from the crisis by implementing strategic adjustments necessary to thrive in a changing industry, and proved that it took innovation, investment and vision to prevail.

4.4 Japan's National Efforts

Japan used to be (it still is albeit in a weakened sense) a highly substantial force in contributing towards semiconductor technology refinement and industry growth. It rose to world leadership in semiconductors under a united national effort, but it stumbled when the internet economy bubble burst. Its journey holds several lessons for China who is facing internal restructuring pressure and external technological suppression.

In the mid-1950s when transistors were applied commercially and integrated circuits were about to set off a revolution in electronics, the Japanese economy began to take off after 10 years of recuperation from its defeat in World War II. In the late 1980s, Japan's GDP was nearing to 2/3 of the US' GDP. Japanese money flowed into the US, purchasing buildings and enterprises and causing lots of misgivings to the world's most powerful country.

The top 10 semiconductor companies in the world were taken up by US firms for a long time after IC was invented, right until the late 1980s. In 1988, the top 10 list was made up of six Japanese companies, three American ones and a Korean one, with the top rank snapped up by Japan's NEC Corporation. Japan's rise to the summit of the science and technology industry started from its robust performance in downstream sectors, notably the textile industry. It then gradually, strenuously and strategically moved to the upstream area, which in this case, was the semiconductor industry.

When Intel met its Waterloo in the early 1980s in its competition with Japanese memory chips manufacturers, the world became curious and intrigued by Japan's seemingly one-stride ascendance to industrial success.

There was an industrial transformation that happened in Japan from 1970 to 1985. During these 15 years, heavy industries such as steel went into a downturn while light and small industries represented by microchips and household appliances started to soar. What was the factor behind this quick and smooth industrial transformation and how did Japan manage to sit at the top of an industry that was widely acknowledged as the most high-grade of all? Research and analysis at that time could not seem to understand Japan, and everyone was either enamored of or intimidated by the "Japanese mode".

There were principally three elements that worked together to create this spectacular Japanese mode. To begin with, America's strategic decision during the Cold War to transfer part of its semiconductor industry to Japan gave Japanese companies the valuable opportunity to learn and to innovate. Second, there was a thriving demand for semiconductor components and systems due to a booming personal computers market in the 1970s and the early 1980s, a time when it seemed the world could never get enough of semiconductors. The third and maybe the most decisive element was a concerted domestic effort between Japan's industry, government and academia to learn from the outside and to create from the inside.

This unity initiated by the Japanese government to establish a technological innovation center consisted of several contending semiconductor enterprises and several state-owned research centers. The collaboration not only brought out teamwork among the three parties but also combined the strengths of different national economy sectors. This element, in particular the VLSIC Technology Research Center supervised by the Ministry of International Trade and Industry (MITI, now known as the Ministry of Economy, Trade and Industry), turned out to be a strategic move in propelling Japan's innovation process and was believed to have paved the way for Japan's semiconductor industry to leap to the forefront.

In 1964, IBM successfully developed the 3rd generation of IC-based computers, stretching the technological gap between the US and Japan even further. Two years later, the MITI officially launched its ultra-high-performance computer development program.

The goal of this program was very clear, that is, to develop a high-performance computer which could stand the competition from IBM, the number one player in the field. As part of its stimulation actions, the MITI gave out a total subsidy of 10 billion yen (US$28 million in 1965) to selected participants in the program. Needless to say, IBM would not stand still and wait to be grabbed by the collar. Instead, it speeded up its R&D pace and released in succession computers that used LSIC and VLSIC. Faced with this tough opponent, the ambitious Japanese government realized that its only opportunity was a real breakthrough in IC core technology.

LSIC and VLSIC were differentiated just by one letter in their names, but this one-letter difference meant a whole new level of fabrication technique and equipment requirement, which involved the use of electron beam or X ray as the light for exposure, the development of new photo resist and extreme precision examine devices, as well as bigger wafer slices and the requisite particulates remove technology, all of which sounded like another world for the Japanese enterprises at that time.

We discussed the overall investment level of world-leading semiconductor companies in previous sections, and it was clear that continuous generous investment was the prerequisite for developing core technology and realizing its consequent economic benefits. For Japanese companies, they were short of both adequate money and sharp positioning. These were the speed bumps the Japanese government, industry and academia were facing.

Japan's solution to stride over the bumps was to gather the money and the vision by bringing different enterprises and research centers together under the same cause. A special committee was set up to conduct specialized and efficient supervision; industry leaders and top semiconductor scientists were summoned to brainstorm strategies and new ideas; and research funds were raised to encourage and subsidize hard-working teams and individuals.

With all preparations done and resources set in motion, the VLSIC Technology Research Program, a milestone in Japan's semiconductor history, was put into action from 1976 to 1979. It was in essence a unanimous and state-leveled collaboration between Japan's government, industry and academia. The largest five semiconductor companies in Japan, namely Fujitsu, Hitachi, Mitsubishi, NEC and Toshiba took up the main mission of the cause. The most advanced research centers in the country, including MITI's Electronic Technology Laboratory, Electronic Research Center and Computer Research Center from Japan's Industrial Technology Research Institute, provided all the equipment and devices necessary for the research. With a total investment of 72 billion yen (US$200 million, of which 40% was contributed by the government and 60% was contributed by the participating companies proportionately), a gathering of the country's smartest scientists and engineers, and a strong resolution to make things happen, Japan set off to develop its own generic core technology for its semiconductor industry.

During the four years of the Program, approximately 1,210 relevant technological patents were applied, among which 347 were credited as commercially credential ones. All the participants in the Program were allowed free access in one form or another to the patents generated from the Program. This sharing mode partly explained the simultaneous rise of a number of Japanese semiconductor companies.

Participants:
Fujitsu, Hitachi,
Mitsubishi, NEC,
Toshiba

Achievements: more than
1,000 technology patents,
developed the world's first
64MB and 256KB dynamic
memory device and posed a
serious threat to US
semiconductor manufacturers

VLSIC
Technology
Research
Program

Strategies: a unanimous
and state–leveled
collaboration between
the government,
industry and academia

Spanning period: 1976–
1979

Investment: 72 billion
yen (US$200 million)

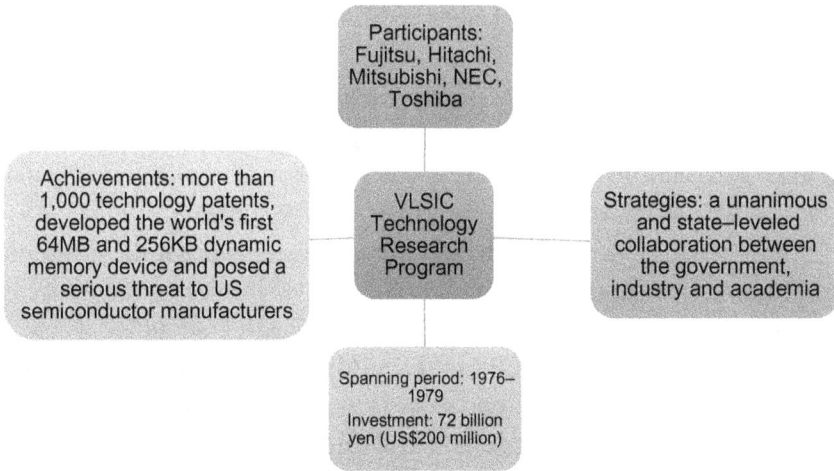

The VLSIC Technology Research Program.

The Program assigned three research teams to focus on three different directions of technology development. The inventions and discoveries from the three contributed to the increase in market share of Japanese photolithography machines and other semiconductor manufacturing equipment. The Reduced Projection Lithography Machine was developed during this time and achieved a steady dominance in the market. Before the 1980s, Japan was obliged to import sophisticated and advanced IC equipment such as photolithography machines from the US. However five years after the implementation of the VLSIC Research Program, Japan was not only self-sufficient with regards to this machine, it also won a global market share bigger than the America's with its self-developed higher-performance Reduced Projection Lithography Machines. In 2000, apart from AMSL from the Netherlands, Japanese companies supplied almost all the advanced lithography machines in the world.

Renewed prospects and strengths were not only seen in Japan's advanced lithography machines, but also in the whole range of semi-conductor manufacturing equipment. This achievement of the Program realized a self-sustainability of relevant semiconductor equipment and boosted the world market share of Japan-manufactured semiconductor devices.

Another industry breakthrough achieved by the Program was the realization of 8 inch wafer production technique, which had been deemed impossible by the industry for some time as it believed the 6 inch wafer was the manufacture limit for monocrystalline silicon wafer. This new technique developed by Japan to make large wafer resulted in a series of technology reforms in the industry.

These remarkable achievements accomplished through the Program served as a force to raise the market position of Japan's semiconductor material manufacturing sector. In 1985, approximately 60% of semiconductor material used around the world were from Japanese companies, and increasesd to 70% two years later. Today, Japan is still a global influence and a force to be reckoned with in the field of semiconductors, which is the real significance of the VLSIC Program.

The Program's 29-billion-yen government investment (US$80 million), which was provided by the MITI, was used as subsidies for researches on generic fundamental technologies. The way MITI spent its money and the technology sharing mode proved critical in motivating all sides to contribute their utmost to the Program. Which company would not want to make full use of such an opportunity sponsored by the government and to ally with other important players in the industry to make breakthroughs in generic fundamental technologies which were going to be shared within themselves freely?

Interestingly, Japan's ability and capacity to make memory chips competitive enough that giants like Intel and Motorola were booted out of the memory market was a by-result of the VLSIC Program. When the five leading participant enterprises of the Program set out to commercialize the technology they developed together, they unexpectedly found that memory chips, instead of processor chips, could benefit the most from their research results. Because of these unexpected combination of circumstances, Japanese companies came to rule in the global memory market (where it took up more than 55% of the market share in the late 1970s and more onwards, whereas in the early 1970s it accounted for no more than 10%) but did not manage to climb much height in the CPU market.

The rewards for Japan's united effort in developing its semiconductor industry were impressive. Surplus began to appear in the industry's international trade in 1979. Trade surplus with the US happened in 1980. Its global market share in semiconductor products surpassed America for a consecutive 10 years after 1986. There were 6 Japanese companies out of the top 10 semiconductor companies in the world, with NEC, Toshiba and Hitachi accounting for the top 3. This "small" country dominated the global semiconductor industry until 1995 when Intel launched its new Pentium microprocessor series and worked with Microsoft to release the new Windows 95 operation system which became the new dominance in the industry.

Japan reaped loads of money from its rising semiconductor industry (an industry, as we mentioned before, that tended to pay back generously if it was invested generously). More significantly, Japan earned the good name and reputation of "Made in Japan", and a big leap in manufacturing standard and capacity stimulated by the advancement in its semiconductors. In America, Japan's rise in the industry posed a severe pressure that spread across sectors ranging from semiconductors to communications to national defense. Such an unfavorable prospect was certainly not envisaged by the US and both government and industry called strongly for counteractions.

The US government accused Japan of unfair competition in the forms of dumping, inappropriate government subsidy, and unfair investment and acquisition activities. It unilaterally imposed high extra tariffs on Japanese goods, such as an absurd 100% on products like computers and televisions. A long and complicated US-Japan semiconductor trade friction began and it only ended when Japan conceded to put a price restraint on all of its exported goods to the US. This compromise made by Japan was the beginning of its fadeout from the top position of the world's semiconductor industry.

4.5 Korea's Journey in Semiconductors

As shown in the previous sections, there is one Korean enterprise — Samsung which always appears in the rankings of the world's semiconductor companies. In Samsung's 2017 second quarter market performance, it claimed a 72% year-on-year growth in net profit and a 17.8% growth in sales volume, demonstrating how robust the company is in the market.

Korea's development in semiconductors is truly an inspiration for latecomers, because the country has taken only a little more than 20 years to start from scratch to move up to the very top of the world's semiconductor ranking. Such a success in such a short time would not be possible without policy support from the Korean government and substantial capital infusion from Korean business tycoons.

It could be traced back to the mid-1960s when Fairchild and Motorola, in order to cut down on their factory labor costs, transferred their semiconductor manufacturing process to Korea. Then in the 1970s, Japanese companies like Toshiba and Sanyo started to build factories in Korea to take over the tasks of Japan's domestic assembly lines. After decades in the role of a labor-intensive assembly room for foreign advanced semiconductor companies who were outsourcing their low-end production, Korea started to develop its own strength in the industry in the late 1970s. With Samsung, LG and Hyundai being the Big Three, Korea's semiconductor industry seemed primitive but promising in certain ways.

The outbreak of the oil crisis in the 1970s drastically altered the global market environment for light industries. Korea's economy growth used to rely on exporting oil-dependent products, but it could no longer continue due to the oil price crisis. It was during this period that big financial groups in Korea such as Samsung began to turn to advanced manufacturing industries like semiconductors.

In 1983, Lee Byung-chul, the founder of Samsung, made a bold decision to invest heavily in memory chips manufacturing. The move was deemed unbelievable to some extent because Lee put in such a large amount of money that if failure should come, he could easily face a total bankruptcy. It turned out to be a blast however. His seemingly insane move eventually made Samsung the number one player in the memory market. For this reason, 1983 was regarded as a turning point for Korea's semiconductor industry.

Lee had a reputation for making unconventional business decisions. As early as in the 1960s when Korea got its first order in outsourcing manufacturing from American semiconductor giants, Lee saw the prospect of an electronics industry in Korea. He began a plan to establish a large industrial park that was going to be bigger in scale than the Sanyo Integrated Electronics Industrial Park, the largest in Japan. For that purpose, he bought more than 200 acres of land in Suwon's suburban area although none of his business partners could see the potential of the land.

While his colleagues' eyes were filled with confusion, Lee's eyes were glistening with promises of the future: miles and miles of industrial land that would provide hundreds of thousands of jobs, generate billions of revenues and lead Korea's hi-tech industry to a new level. He did not think that the place was large at all; as a matter of fact, he thought it was not big enough to accommodate future capacities which he was so sure would materialize someday.

The construction of the Samsung Industrial Park in Suwon was completed in the late 1960s. The park started as an OEM factory for Japanese enterprises who were very protective of their core technologies from the keen Samsung employees. Lee knew very well about Japan's secrecy and prudence, but he also knew that if he could get his hands on the fundamental technologies, it could ultimately mean an increased market share for Samsung. Therefore, he started to invest heavily in research and development, which was pivotal in pushing the company to the forefront of the global electronics industry.

Lee's series of bold decisions came from his shrewd observations and his entrepreneurial vision. Since Japan's economy took off on a high-speed semiconductor train in the late 1970s, he had been contemplating on Japan's successes and frequently consulted Japanese academics and industrial leaders for advice. Inaba Shuzo, the famous economist, one of the main designers of Japan's after-war resurrection and a believer that semiconductors would be the main opportunity for future economic growth and global power competition, gave assurance to Lee to march into the promising industry.

Lee chose the already oversupplied 64 kilobyte DRAM memory chips market as an entry point into the industry. It was a tough decision and he was only allowed to succeed. On 14th March 1983, the self-made and hugely successful businessman dialed the number of *JoongAng Ilbo* after a night of thinking and rethinking. He told the *JoongAng Ilbo*,

Lee Byung-chul, the founder of Samsung.

the most influential newspaper in Korea, to announce to the public Samsung's decision to launch an unprecedented semiconductor project. His strategy was to push other players out and win the market by waging a relentless price war.

Several supporting forces were behind Samsung's semiconductor project. The Korean government gave the most assurance to Lee. To start with, there were preferential industrial laws and regulations compiled specially to create a business-friendly environment for domestic semiconductors. The government also placed big orders with domestic semiconductor companies and executed tariff protection policies to raise the odds of companies like Samsung.

In particular, the Korean government ordered 8,360 personal computers from its domestic market in 1982, when there were altogether no more than 1,000 personal computers across the country. This stimulation from the top proved very effective to the domestic demand for semiconductor components. Personal computers received a 10-fold increase in demand one year later in 1983. Additionally, the Korean government provided great financial support by appropriating the war indemnity it received from Japan in 1965. It gave US$346 million worth of governmental loans from the indemnity to its semiconductor companies. It also successfully lobbied big consortiums to raise US$2 billion worth of private investments for the industry.

After getting all the external support it could acquire, Samsung began to take further actions towards its ultimate target. The 64 kilobyte DRAM patents and technology were purchased from the Japanese company Micron, which was in a serious capital crisis and urgently needed to trade for cash. The manufacturing equipment was ordered from the Japanese company Sharp. With the technology and equipment needed for research and production in place, and a rich experience in reverse engineering, Samsung began to realize an incremental innovation and take off on the fast lane of development.

Personnel was another strategic resource that Samsung was pursuing for its cause. Lee used his personal charisma and persuasive skills to enlist the service of able men, particularly Korean scientists and engineers who worked for American companies. Morris Chang, the founder of TSMC, was wooed to join Samsung before leaving the US to start his own business in Taiwan. The pursuit came to naught of course.

In 1984, Samsung launched its 64 kilobyte DRAM chips, which unfortunately coincided with a downturn caused by overcapacity in the global semiconductor industry. The market price of a memory chip plummeted from US$4 to US$0.30 within eight months. Samsung's manufacturing costs for each chip stood at US$1.30, which meant that they were to be sold with a 1-dollar deficit. The market recession forced Intel, once the leader in the global memory market, to withdraw and Japanese companies to largely cut down on their investment in the memory sector. Samsung moved against the tide like a crazy gambler, and continued its investment in expanding manufacturing capacity and developing memory chips with larger storage systems. At the end of 1986, Samsung's total loss reached US$300 billion, with an empty equity capital.

As money was being thrown away, Lee had to face endless complaints and frustration about how deep a deficit the company was in and how hopeless the outlook was, if there were no immediate remedies to be taken. A bankruptcy was looming for Samsung.

Despite all these, Lee did not call for a halt. More investment, more development and more capacity were put in. He believed in his judgement and his anti-cycle strategy. Samsung would increase capacity in times of bad market and languid price, and wait for competitors to knuckle under the pressure. Then it would be the winner and have an absolute say on the market and the price.

Lee survived the recession and emerged a winner. The trade deal struck between Japan and the US brought back the price of memory chips and Samsung was one of the few who held out with a remarkable capacity. Orders and profits began to flow in and the gambler Lee was rewarded with success. In 1992, Samsung surpassed NEC to become the world's largest memory chips manufacturer. Actually, Korea had learned from Japan how to wield the price strategy to beat down competitors and to win over market share; the student had in turn brought its teacher down.

After this hard-earned victory, the anti-cycle strategy became a powerful and frequently used weapon in Samsung's global battlefield. Memory chip manufacturers in the world declared bankruptcy one after another as Samsung played the same efficient strategy to uphold itself as the absolute industry leader. In 1998, Korea took the place of Japan to become the world's largest supplier of memory chips. This shift had taken 15 years to materialize. It all started in 1983 when Lee made up his mind to risk his fortune in semiconductors. Samsung has held this top rank right until today.

An article in *The Economist* attributed Korea's success in the manufacturing industry in the 1980s to its domestic preferential policies which gathered a large number of resources and tilt them towards several powerful financial groups. With such green passes in policies and powerful support in resources including money, these groups were able to venture into the capital-intensive semiconductor industry and withstand the heavy and inevitable financial losses of the first few years.

It should also be noted that the semiconductor trade clash between the US and Japan, which resulted in increased tariffs and higher export prices, opened up opportunities for Korean enterprises to enter the market. Korea's example once again proved that developments in the semiconductor industry could drive up other high-tech industry sectors. Thanks to the large-scale investment of companies like Samsung and Hyundai (renamed as SK Hynix) under the encouragement and support of the Korean government in a critical international climate, Korea's manufacturing industry took off and led the development of Asian countries in the following decades.

4.6 TSMC, the World's First Dedicated Semiconductor Foundry

Almost at the same time when Japan surpassed the US to dominate the global semiconductor industry and Korea took the place of Japan in the memory chip market, a Taiwanese company was creating a new business mode in in the semiconductor industry. TSMC made full use of the cheap labor force in East Asia and invented a new foundry model in the industrial chain.

In 1985, 54-year-old Morris Chang left the US after 30 years of high-ranking positions in several well-known US semiconductor companies. He returned to Taiwan to take charge of of industrial and technological developments. Two years later, with the support of the Taiwanese government, he founded TSMC in Hsinchu Science and Industrial Park as the world's first dedicated independent semiconductor foundry. In this model, TSMC would only be manufacturing devices for other companies but would not be designing them. Thus it would never compete directly in the market and could scale its production capacity to a customer's needs.

TSMC set the example and standard for pure-play semiconductor foundries in a period when firms increasingly saw value in outsourcing their manufacturing capacity to Asia. After TSMC, a new and more efficient labor division mode in the semiconductor industrial chain came into being, and new dedicated foundries started to spring up. This new model promoted specialization in the industry and contributed to further prosperity in the semiconductor industry.

Before leaving the US, Chang spent 25 years at Texas Instruments where he rose up the ranks to become the group's Vice President. He also spent two years at General Instrument Corporation as President and Chief Operating Officer. He was born in Ningbo, Zhejiang (mainland China's east coast area) in 1931, and spent his youth in various

TSMC headquarters in Hsinchu, Taiwan.

places during the Japanese invasion and the Chinese civil war. His family moved to Hong Kong in 1948 and he moved to the United States to attend Harvard University the following year. He transferred to MIT one year later and received his bachelor's and master's degrees in mechanical engineering there.

He joined Texas Instruments in 1958 when the company was rapidly rising in its field. After three years, he became manager of the engineering section and was later appointed as Vice President responsible for the company's worldwide semiconductor business.

Originally, microelectronic devices were manufactured by companies that both designed and produced the devices. It was necessary because the manufacturing process involved tweaking parameters, precise understanding of the process and the occasional need to redesign. Therefore, these manufacturers were involved in both the research and development of the manufacturing process and the research and development of microcircuit design. However, as manufacturing techniques developed, microelectronic devices became more standardized. This allowed design to be split from manufacture. Seeing this separation trend between manufacture and design, Chang saw value in the foundry model which could optimize productivity. Hence, he founded TSMC to concentrate on fabricating and testing the physical microelectronic products.

For the newly-started foundry factory to start mass production, Chang needed expert personnel, manufacturing technology and contract orders from leading fabless firms in the world. For that purpose, he enlisted the help of the president of General Electric's semiconductor department, and successfully landed an order from Intel after acquiring all the relevant technology licensing. An episode happened during this first cooperation between Intel and TSMC and it spoke well of Chang's unwavering determination and the factory's trustworthiness. Andrew Grove, CEO of Intel, wanted to step back from the deal after his inspection of TSMC revealed certain disqualifications in the manufacturing process. Chang, however, provided guarantee of TSMC's reliability by diminishing the flaws within weeks and won back Grove's heart.

Gradually, leading fabless semiconductor companies around the world realized that TSMC was the fastest among Japanese, Singaporean and Korean foundry companies to deliver orders. The Taiwanese company thus began to manufacture for most of the leading microchip design companies, including Qualcomm, Nvidia, AMD, Media Tek, Marvell, Intel, Texas Instruments and Broadcom. TSMC's rise to the leading position in the field was a combined result of capitalizing on the impending industrial transformation and constant upgrading of its manufacturing and management capacities. TMSC's success was just a chapter in the big story of the industrial transformation that took place in the latter half of the 20th century, but it heralded the beginning of wafer foundry as an independent and substantial industrial chain in the semiconductor industry.

Besides Japan's and Korea's governmental support for their national semiconductor industries, the Taiwanese government's role in TSMC's success was also instrumental. In the early 1970s, Taiwan began to purchase technology from Radio Corporation of America (RCA) for its own research and development program. After some re-innovated technology was developed in the Electronic Research Center of Taiwan Industry Institution, the government began to coordinate the collaboration of TSMC and another company called UMC (United Microelectronics Corporation), to whom it handed over the technology. The Taiwanese government participated actively in several of its leading semiconductor companies until the late 1980s. It was only when they began to see profitability did the government feel confident to leave the matters to the hands of able entrepreneurs.

In 1997 when TSMC was listed in the New York Stock Exchange, the company saw an annual revenue of US$1.3 billion and a net profit of US$535 million. In 2009, when Chang returned to the position of TSMC's CEO after he stepped back in 2005, the company started to invest heavily in the microelectronic manufacturing technique. It then pioneered the 40 nanometer and 28 nanometer techniques, making itself a counterpart of Samsung and Intel in IC manufacturing technology.

As the symbol of Taiwan's high-tech industry and the epitome of Taiwan's economic development, TSMC became the world's largest wafer foundry company in 2013 with a 46% global market share and a US$1.99 billion revenue.

Significant events in the development history of semiconductors.

Year	Events
1947	William Shockley, Walter Brattain and John Bardeen invented the world's first point-contact transistor.
1948	Bell Labs developed the technique to produce single crystalline germanium.
1949	The California-based IC manufacturer International Rectifier launched the first commercially available semiconductor components in history.
	Claude Shannon (1916–2001), "the father of information theory", published the first article centered on the programming of a computer for playing chess and using the computer to solve the game.
1950	Bipolar junction transistor (BJT) was commercially available for a series of consumer products.
1951	The world's first commercial computer was delivered to the US Census Bureau.

(Continued)

Year	Events
1952	One year after its emergence, Texas Instruments started to focus on semiconductor business.
	Motorola started its research and development laboratory in Phoenix, Arizona, to research new solid-state technology on commercial high-power germanium-based transistor.
	IBM launched IBM 701 Electronic Data Processing Machine, its first commercial scientific computer.
1953	Motorola received its first semiconductor technology patent which involved its newly developed, lower-cost transistors used to assist wireless communication signal reception and automobile audio power transformation.
1954	Texas Instruments and Industrial Development Engineering Associates (I.D.E.A.) worked together to design and manufacture the first transistor radio.
	Texas Instruments created the first workable silicon transistor.
1955	The first fully transistorized computer which used discrete transitions instead of vacuum tubes was developed.
	Bell Labs developed photoresist material.
	William Shockley left Bell Labs to work on new silicon-based semiconductor devices and opened the first semiconductor company, Shockley Semiconductor Laboratory one year later in Mountain View, California. His attempts to commercialize a new transistor design led to California's "Silicon Valley" becoming a hotbed of electronics innovation.
1956	General Motors launched the first solid-state silicon switch.
1957	Transistors were used in America's first satellite, Explorer 1.
	The traitorous eight led by Robert Noyce left Shockley Semiconductor Laboratory and founded Fairchild Semiconductor under the sponsorship of Sherman Fairchild, founder of Fairchild Aircraft and Fairchild Camera.
	The sales volume of the semiconductor industry exceeded US$100 million for the first time.
	Seymour Cray (1925–1996) developed the first fully transistorized supercomputer.
1958	Jack Kilby invented the first germanium integrated circuit.
	The US Air Force started to apply semiconductor technology to design its transcontinental ballistic missile.
1959	US National Semiconductor was established in Danbury, Connecticut.
	Robert Noyce invented a silicon version of the integrated circuit and Jean Hoerni developed the associated fabrication technique called planar process which made the IC truly practical in the manufacturing industry.

References

1. Everett M. Rogers. *Silicon Valley Fever: Growth of High-technology Culture* [M]. 1985.
2. Andrew Grove. *Only the Paranoid Survive: How to Exploit the Crisis Points That Challenge Every Company* [M]. 1999.
3. Yu Wenxin. *The Samsung Empire* [M]. Beijing: Modern Press. 2014.
4. Wu Jun. *On the Wave Top* [M]. Beijing: Posts and Telecom Press. 2016.
5. Wu Jun. *The Legend of Silicon Valley.* Beijing: Posts and Telecom Press. 2016.
6. Wei Yanan. *Science for the Whole Human Being.* People's Daily. 1984.
7. Zhou Cheng. *Case Study on the Technology Innovation League Cooperated Between Japanese Government, Industry and Academia* [J]. China Computer Science. 2008.
8. Tong Shibai. *Looking Back into the 20th Century: In Commemoration of the Invention of Transistors.* Journal of Electrical and Electronic Education. 2001.
9. Bi Yanian. *The Story of Morris Chuang, the Founder of TSMC* [J]. Chinese Entrepreneurship. 2016.
10. Linda Shu. *The Leader of Global Semiconductors: Intel* [M]. Shanghai University of Finance and Economics Press. 2007.

Chapter 5

The Journey of China's Microchips

Overture

China missed out on a historic opportunity to develop semiconductors in the 1970s, and it has been paying a great cost since. Technological progress can be so revolutionary and disruptive that every step backward can result in a bigger gap to be overcome in the long run.

In the mid-1960s, the newly-found Republic of China started to gain momentum in the industry. After a 10-year domestic upheaval, a series of national plans was devoted to developing computer science and semiconductor technology. Recently, increasing pressure from the US prodded China to double up its effort to get rid of its dependency on foreign semiconductor technology.

China's progress in building an indigenous semiconductor industry has been slow, but the country is in it for the long run.

> **Nay, it was better, to meet some dangers half way, though they come nothing near, than to keep too long a watch upon their approaches; for if a man watches too long, it is odds he will fall asleep.**
>
> **— Francis Bacon, *Of Delay***

5.1 Pioneers in China's Semiconductor Industry

In this chapter, the first two sections will retrace the difficult journeys and remarkable achievements of pioneers in China's semiconductor industry after 1949 when the country's civil war ended. We will recap the big events and the general timeline of China's semiconductor development history. China in the 1950s and especially in the early 1960s had kept a close pace with the world's leading companies in the industry. It was achieved by a common national effort and the devotion of some scientists who chose to return to China from the West to contribute to their newly-found nation. This patriotism and responsibility, often at the expense of a more promising and prosperous individual future, was witnessed and praised by many people. It was this sense of sacrifice and dedication that catapulted many Third World countries out of their backwardness.

1. *Huang Kun, the Founder of China's Semiconductor Physics Discipline*

Huang Kun (黄昆, 1919–2005) was a Chinese physicist and a founding member of the CAS. He was awarded the State Preeminent Science and Technology Award, the highest science award in China, by President Jiang Zemin in 2001.

Born in Beijing, China in 1919, Huang graduated from Yenching University with a degree in physics in 1941. During his school days, Yenching University was forced to move to Kunming in Yunnan province because of war. There he befriended two persons who were going to leave their names in the history of physics, just as he did. They were Yang Zhenning (winner of the 1957 Nobel Prize in Physics) and Zhang Shoulian (an Institute of Electrical and Electronics Engineers fellow). The three of them were known as the three Musketeers of the physics college as they were constantly engaged in endless and fierce discussions about physics problems. According to Yang, there was once when they quarreled throughout the whole night in order to figure out the definition of "measurement" in quantum mechanics. As Yang recalled, Huang was obsessed with every detail and would not give up looking for supporting materials to back up his ideas. Many years from then, they still considered that period of time when they were utterly absorbed in resolving their common puzzles as the most unforgettable and valuable period in their lives.

Huang Kun graduated from Yenching University in 1941.

In 1948, he earned his PhD from the H. H. Wills Physics Lab of Bristol University in England. He continued his postdoctoral studies at Liverpool University, where he co-authored the book, *Dynamical Theory of Crystal Lattices* with Max Born, the German Nobel laureate. The book became a classic work of modern physics. The Born–Huang Approximation, which provided an important inspiration for the invention of integrated circuits, was named after the two authors.

During his six years' stay in England, he was very much concerned about his motherland's fate. He saw himself tightly bound to the future of his country, as evidenced from his letters to Yang who was pursuing a PhD at Chicago University in the US.

One of his letters to Yang read like this: "Sometimes, when I tell people that I'm going back to China in one or two years, they seem quite puzzled, as if something is wrong with me; why I would choose to jump into troubled waters instead of settling down in an orderly and

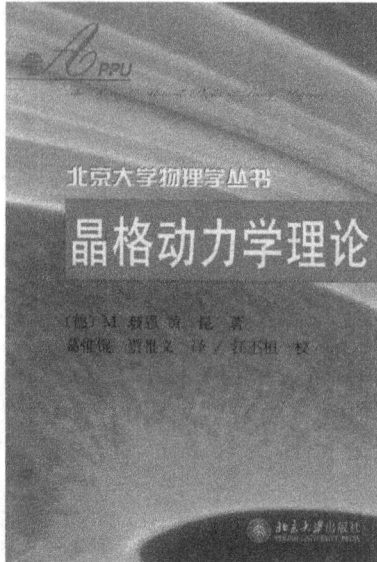

Dynamical Theory of Crystal Lattices.

secure land. Truly, I don't know how much of a difference we, nothing but a scholar, can bring to the future of our country... But if we stay here, in this orderly and secure land, just for the purpose of avoiding the hard time that is to come, then we've failed the expectations our country has placed on us. We are not taught and raised by our country so that one day we can walk away when it faces a grave crisis; we are taught and raised to make a difference, however small it is."

This deep concern and ingrained responsibility Huang had for China's future determined his choice several years later and his journey in the following half century. His American counterparts at that time were faced with no such definite choices between individual fulfillment and patriotic duty. They were able to submerge themselves into the research and development of new technologies and inventions. As mentioned earlier, the transistor was invented around this time and a new era of semiconductors was heralded in which integrated circuits and minicomputers were about to transform the world.

In 1951, as his choice led him, Huang returned to China to become a professor of physics at Peking University. This was a time when China had just emerged from decades of devastating war and was yearning for revitalization in every sector. Giving up his ongoing research projects in Britain, Yang took up the mission of developing China's physics discipline and high-end physics personnel and started his 26 years of teaching life.

He was popular with students at Peking University. They imagined this relatively established PhD who just came back from Britain as an elderly sir. So, when the new physics teacher walked into the classroom with a vivacious 30-year-old demeanor and talked in his Peking-accented Mandarin, an agreeable impression was left in the minds of his students. He then secured their fondness and respect towards the discipline with his expertise in the field and his enthusiasm in delivering his lessons.

He later chaired the University's Solid-state Physics Teaching and Research Center and established a more efficient and sound teaching system. In 1954, he launched China's first semiconductor physics course in the University. Famous alumni of the course included CAS academicians like Gan Ziqian, Qin Guogang and Xia Jianbai. His books, *Solid-state Physics* (1966) and *Semiconductor Physics* (1958, co-authored with Xie Xide), were widely celebrated for their clarity and insights. They remained as perennial items in science students' and researchers' booklists.

In 1956, Huang was commissioned by the Chinese central government under the leadership of Premier Zhou Enlai to coordinate and direct a national program on semiconductor research and development. In 1977, Deng Xiaoping appointed him as the Director of the Semiconductor Institution of CAS. During this period of his career, Huang set up the first semiconductor super-lattice laboratory in China and started a new exploration in material science and solid-state physics. He made many groundbreaking contributions, with the Born-Huang Approximation being one of them. His career in physics intertwined with China's ambition in science development and he witnessed a nation's long journey from ground zero.

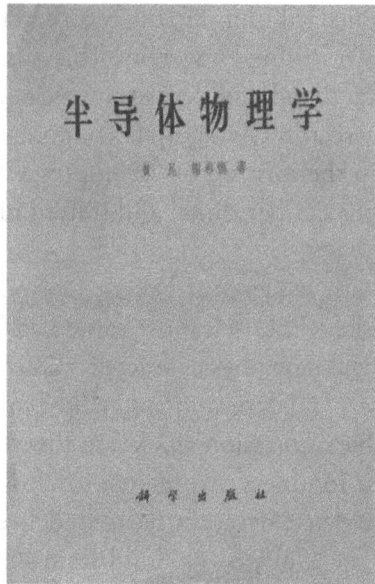

Semiconductor Physics.

2. *Wang Shouwu, a Pioneer in Semiconductor Devices*

The success of China's first GaAs laser, first 4 kilobyte and 16 kilobyte DRAM microchips and the development and improvement of LSIC mass production could be attributed to Wang Shouwu. A physicist, scientist and engineer, he shared a similar experience as Huang Kun and many others, who, despite all odds, left the West to return to their motherland to make a difference.

Wang Shouwu (王守武, 1919–2014) was a native of Xuzhou, Jiangsu province. He graduated from Tongji University in 1941 and received his master's degree in 1946 and doctor's degree in 1949 from Purdue University in the US. He was a researcher at the Institute of Semiconductor of the CAS. He was also the honorary director of the Microelectronics Center of the CAS.

Starting from 1963, Wang was devoted to the research of GaAs lasers. He created a simple optical method to easily determine the crystal orientation and contributed to the success of the first GaAs laser in China. This achievement was as exciting as the success of China's first monocrystalline germanium and silicon boule in 1957 and 1958.

Wang Shouwu and his wife at Purdue University in 1949.

Wang established the first transistor factory in China in 1958 and was the director of the factory from 1980 to 1985. It was called the 109 Semiconductor Factory of CAS, which later became the Microelectronics Center of CAS. He led research staff to study how to enhance the rate of finished products of LSIC, resulting in remarkably improved rates of finished products and cost. The 4 kilobyte and 16 kilobyte DRAM microchips were the results of his efforts.

Our Responsibilities Now and in the Future

(Written by Wang Shouwu in his 5th year of primary school in 1930 and published in a newspaper.)

My friends, do you not know how much danger our country is in right now? It is wavering on a narrow rope, exposed to the bellowing wind and the slashing rain, without adequate shelter and confident defense. Its outlook has never been darker.

To bring our country back into a position of safety and stability, a series of capable and wise men have tried their upmost and risked their lives. Shouldn't

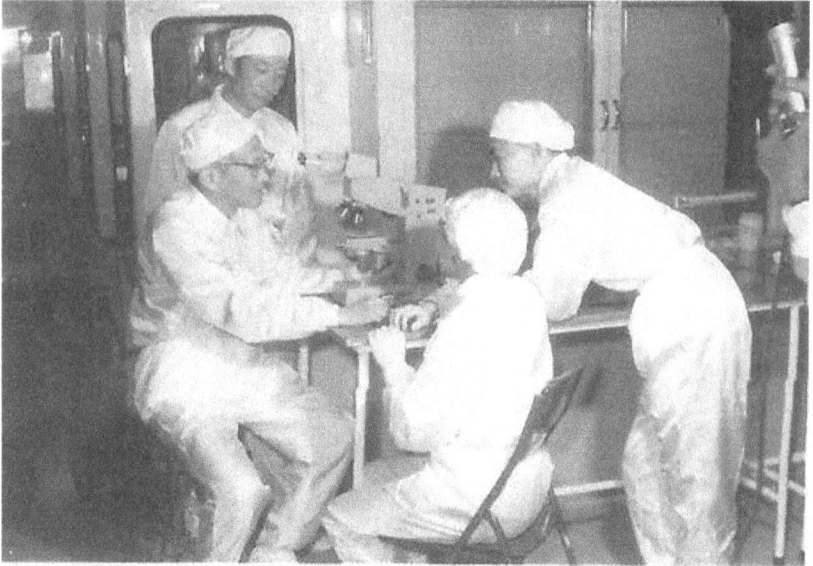

Wang Shouwu working in a cleanroom with his colleagues in 1979.

we, our generation and the generations to come, take on the responsibility, now and in the future? Yes, we should, in every reason we have.

Years and decades from now, our roles would shift from being students to being the mainstay of our country's strength and confidence. But are we ready for that? Can we accomplish this major transition? What a force can we prove ourselves to be for our country?

We will only get to the positive answers if we work hard now to pursue truth and science, and to equip ourselves with what is needed to lift China out of this danger and uncertainty.

My friends, China's future will be our future too. We must be poised to fight for the future and the brightness of our country, more than we would do for ourselves.

5.2 Distinguished Females in the Field

In this section, we want to pay tribute to the females who broke out of traditional expectations and viewpoints of women, demanded no less of themselves than men had and achieved remarkable and respectable accomplishments in China's semiconductor science.

1. *Xie Xide, the First Female President in a Major Comprehensive University in China*

Xie Xide (谢希德, 1921–2000), also known as Hsi-teh Hsieh and Hilda Hsieh, was President of Fudan University from 1983 to 1989. She was a well-known solid-state physicist, educational leader, social activist, fellow of the 3rd World Academy of Sciences and a key figure in the development of China's educational relations with the international community. She made prominent contributions to the development of China's higher education and science research.

Xie Xide in her youth.

She was born on 19th March 1921 in the port city of Quanzhou in Fujian, southeastern China, into a family that valued education. Her father Xie Yuming had a PhD in physics from the University of Chicago and was a classmate of Yang Zhenning's father. He taught in Yenching University for many years. Under her father's influence, Xie was greatly motivated and started her long journey of researching into physics at a young age.

Xie was not in good health when she was young. Due to a serious knee joint tuberculosis disease suffered when she was 17, she was bedridden for four years before enrolling at Xiamen University, one of China's most prestigious educational institutions. After the disease, she had difficulty walking and running as she could not bend her right leg. Xie was also diagnosed with breast cancer in her middle age. She was not held back by her ailing health though, not when she was 17 and not when she was 60. In her later years, she had to stand while doing work because of the problem of her leg. When she could stand no more after being hit by a heart failure and a respiratory failure, she turned her hospital ward into her work office.

Xie spent much of her youth in Beijing and did her undergraduate studies at Xiamen University. She obtained her master's degree in physics from Smith College and received a PhD in physics from MIT.

In 1951, Xie and her husband Cao Tianqin (a doctorate degree holder from Cambridge University, member of CAS and pioneer of China's protein research) kept their promises and chose to return to China. However, the process was not so easy. The American government did not allow Chinese science and engineering students to return to their own country due to the outbreak of war in the Korean Peninsula. The quick-witted woman came up with a reasonable excuse to leave America. They went to England, where they held their wedding ceremony, and finally arrived back at China.

Xie's career as a scientist and university leader began in Shanghai when she was appointed as a lecturer in the Department of Physics at Fudan University. In 1956, she became an associate professor. In 1958, she served as Adjunct Director for the Shanghai Institute of Technical Physics of CAS. In 1968, she served as Director of the Institute of Modern Physics at Fudan University, and was elected President of the University five years later. After her tenure ended in 1988, she was appointed Advisor of the University until her passing.

Xie was responsible for the organization of China's first professional team focused on the research of semiconductors when she was transferred to Peking University in 1956. She spent a whole year researching material while cooperating with another noted physicist, Huang Kun, to jointly publish China's first book on semiconductors. She was the founder and inventor of several scientific disciplines, including self-conductor physics and surface physics. She made great contributions to the fields of surface and interface physics as well as the theoretical study of electronic properties in quantum devices and heterojunction structures.

Xie also nurtured several top semiconductor scientists in China and made contributions to the construction and development of physics-related scientific and research institutions. She facilitated international exchange and cooperation in scientific fields while undertaking tasks with the Chinese Physical Society. She helped to set up the Fudan University's Centre for American Studies. She received honorary doctorates from 12 universities worldwide, including the US, UK, Japan, Canada, Hong Kong and China. John Bardeen, the co-inventor of transistors, founder of the Bardeen–Cooper–Schrieffer theory and a two-time winner of the Nobel Prize in Physics, praised Xie as a key figure in China's scientific development while visiting Fudan University in the 1980s.

2. *Lin Lanying, the Mother of Semiconductor Materials in China*

Lin Lanying (林兰英, 1918–2003) was credited as the "mother of aerospace materials" and the "mother of semiconductor materials" in China. Her many contributions included producing China's first monocrystalline silicon and the first mono-crystal furnace used to extract silicon. Her work laid the foundation for the development of microelectronics and optoelectronics in China.

Lin was born in Putian city, Fujian province in southern China. At the age of 6, she fought a battle against her family, which was deeply influenced by Chinese social norms and thought girls would be better off not to attend schools, so that she could be allowed to get an education. As she was required to do all the washing and cooking in the family, she often had to work on her school tasks till 12 midnight. Despite this, she earned a scholarship every semester.

She continued her study at Fukien Christian University, a top university at that time in China, and earned a bachelor's degree in physics as one of the best in her class. After 8 years of working at the university, during which she compiled her first book *Course for Experiments in Optics* and earned recognition as a professor, she applied to attend Dickinson College in the US and was granted a full scholarship. After she earned another bachelor's degree in mathematics from Dickinson College, she went on to study solid-state physics at the University of Pennsylvania. She thought that compared with math, physics was more applicable and more useful for China. In 1955, she received a doctorate degree in solid-state physics, becoming the first Chinese national and the first female in the history of the University to earn a doctorate degree.

Lin Lanying in her doctorate gown.

Lin wanted to return to China after graduation, but many Chinese students were not allowed to leave at that time. She instead went to work at Sylvania Company through the recommendation of her professor at the University of Pennsylvania. Her job was a senior engineer focusing on the manufacture of semiconductors. The company had failed several times in making monocrystalline silicon. Lin discovered the hinge problems and helped the company to successfully engineer the silicon technology.

Thanks to a treaty signed by the Chinese government during the Geneva Conference in 1956 that covered its international students, Lin was able to return to China at the beginning of 1957. Just before she boarded the ship, the US Federal Bureau of Investigation approached her and threatened to withhold her earnings of US$6,800 for that year, so as to persuade her to stay. Lin accepted the withholding of her salary and boarded the ship to return to China.

After her return, she became a researcher at the Institute of Physics of CAS and then moved to the Institute of Semiconductor of CAS and spent her research life there. Her first accomplishment was making the first monocrystalline silicon in China. By virtue of her working experience in Sylvania Company, she had first-hand knowledge of the monocrystalline silicon technique, but she could not get her hands on necessary equipment and materials because of embargoes from other countries. She worked out adjustments to the process and successfully fabricated monocrystalline silicon in 1958, making China the third country to master the technique. In 1962, she designed the mono-crystal furnace, which was licensed to many countries. In the same year, she started to develop extensive silicon materials in high-purified vapor phase and liquid phase and made the first monocrystalline GaAs in China. Lin's GaAs achieved the highest mobility in the world and led China to become the world leader in the field. With the successful manufacture of this new material, China's research and development on military monitoring devices, artificial satellites and atomic bombs were able to reach new levels. This contribution led Lin to be named as the "mother of aerospace materials".

3. *Xia Peisu, the Mother of Computer Science in China*

Xia Peisu (夏培肃, 1923–2014), a renowned computer scientist and educator, was the chief designer of China's first general-purpose digital computer. A professor of the Institute of Computing Technology at CAS, she devoted her whole life to scientific research and enjoyed a prolific and distinguished career.

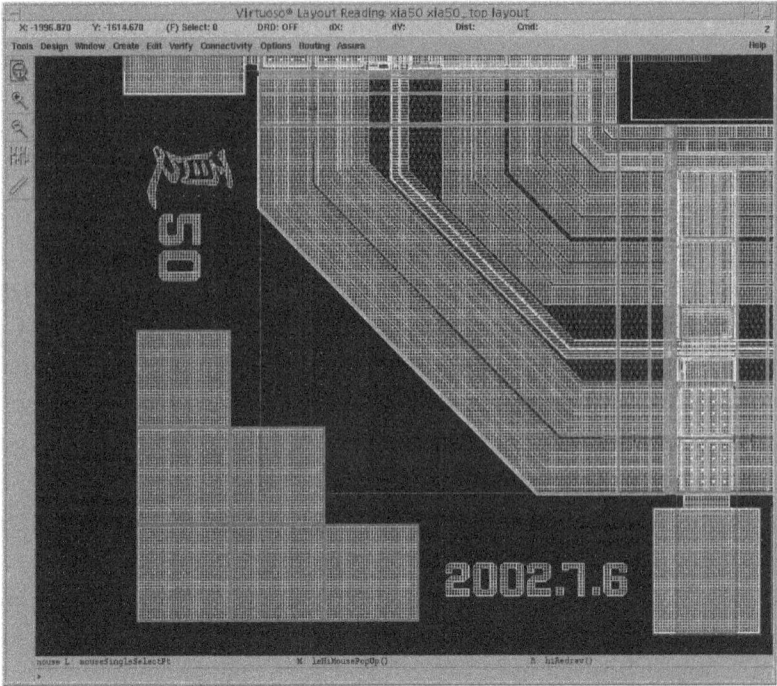

Loongson I microchip inscribed with "夏50" to commemorate the 50th year of Xia's dedicated service to China's computer science.

Born into a family of teachers in southwest China's Chongqing municipality in 1923, Xia developed sound foundations in ancient Chinese prose and mathematics while growing up. She clinched top positions in mathematics in her class and was admitted into Chongqing National Central University (which was renamed Nanjing University in 1949) to study engineering, as she aspired to save the country from the claws of Japanese invaders. In October 1945, Xia was recommended for admission to the Telecommunication Research Institute of National Chiao Tung University in Chongqing to pursue her postgraduate study. Only two females was admitted into the Institute before 1949 and she was one of them.

Two years later, Xia passed her examinations and became a doctoral candidate of the Department of Electrical Engineering at the University of Edinburgh in Britain to study electric circuitry theory, automation, nonlinear ordinary differential equations and their applications. She earned her doctorate degree in July 1950 and continued her research as a Post-Doc researcher in Britain. In the autumn of 1951, she returned to China with her husband Yang Liming (an academician of CAS and a well-known nuclear physicist).

During her one year in the Laboratory of Telecommunication Network of the Department of Electrical Engineering at Tsinghua University, four years in the Institute of Mathematics at CAS and the Institute of Modern Physics at CAS, and a life-long research career in the Institute of Computing Technology at CAS, she achieved many "firsts" in the early development history of China's computer science.

Together with Min Naida and Wang Chuanying, she was enlisted into the first electronic computer research team in China in 1952 by Professor Hua Luogeng, president of the Institute of Mathematics at CAS. In 1956, after overcoming various difficulties in acquiring necessary resources, Xia and her colleagues started to do tests on fundamental logic circuits and mapped out the overall technical outline for developing electronic computers in China. The book she wrote at this time, *Principles of Electronic Computer,* is the first textbook in its field in China. In this book, the Chinese translations of many computer terminologies and concepts were first introduced and are still used today. She participated in the founding of China's first Institute of Computing Technology (ICT), which was one of the Four National Emergency Response Measures brought up by Premier Zhou Enlai. In 1958, she led the design of China's first general-purpose digital computer, Machine 107, demonstrating that China had the capability of designing and building its own computers.

The success of Machine 107 was highly praised and it became a nationwide inspiration. Before this, China suffered a critical shortage of materials and resources for developing its own electronic computer, such as having no books to introduce computer theory systematically and comprehensively. To solve that problem, Xia and her colleagues pulled every strings they had to collect relevant English journals from domestic libraries and took every chance to ask foreign friends to look out for the materials they needed but could not get their hands on.

Xia Peisu.

China's research in computer science was conducted under such diffi-culties that Xia was the only one of the three-member team to hold out until the end, as Wang changed his profession to study atomic energy in the Soviet Union in 1955 and Min moved to Germany in 1958.

After the success of 107, Xia proposed the Maximum Time Difference Pipeline theory, which significantly boosted computer performance by reducing the clock cycle of a pipelined computer. The high-speed array processor she designed was achieved in a low cost way by using alternative materials in the face of an embargo of similar products by the US. It also broke the performance ceiling laid by the US. This achievement gener-ated considerable impacts in the world and made great contributions to oil exploration in China. She also led the research and development work on functionally distributed computer systems and successfully delivered the GF10 series of computers, which later became one of the key research projects in the Institute of Computing Technology for a long period.

Machine 107 developed by Xia Peisu's team.

Xia envisioned as early as in the 1980s that the development and application of high performance computers (HPC) was of paramount importance to China's national competitiveness. While pushing forward HPC-related research activities, she also proposed that China should vigorously promote the design and fabrication of VLSIC, otherwise its fortune would be determined by others. Her students, including two winners of the National Outstanding Doctoral Dissertations and three winners of the China Youth Science and Technology Awards, made remarkable contributions to the research and development of HPC and VLSIC.

Zhu Mingfa was a postgraduate student of Xia in 1979. He joined her in the National High-tech Research and Development Program in 1986 (also known as the 863 Program) to work on a series of Dawning computers. As the chief architect, his work included directing the development of the Dawning-1000 HPC and Lenovo Deepcom-1800/6800 super computer. He later became a member of the CAS. Li Guojie, also a member of the CAS and a student of Xia, served as the director of ICT and founded Dawning Technology Corporation. He was a key figure in China's HPC industry and a major architect in developing Loongson microchip.

Xia trained more than 700 computer professionals during her tenure as the technology lead for the computer training programs in China's first Institute of Computer Technology. These people later became the leaders of computer research and development in China. She set a high standard for her students on research and on moral values, not only through her persuasive and patient words but also through her personal example.

5.3 When Did the Wide Gap Start?

In the first two years after the Republic of China was founded, the names mentioned in the previous two sections had not returned from overseas studies. There was almost no domestic capacity for manufacturing and research in semiconductors. Only a few factories existed and no more than 1,000 machine tools were in operation in the country. China yearned for qualified scientists to return and technology support from its allies.

In October 1952, the second China-Soviet commercial talk was held in Moscow. One of the main agendas of the Chinese delegation was to get Soviet Union's support in building factories to manufacture electronic tubes, switch machines and other wireless electronic components. The Soviet Union, being one of the two most powerful countries in the world, agreed to help build China's vacuum tubes and switch machines factory. However, it did not agree to be involved with issues concerning wireless electronic components manufacturing. Without this, the other two components would not work out either. Soviet Union itself depended on Eastern Germany's technology and personnel support for its components factories, and China needed to seek help from there too.

After talks and negotiations, Eastern Germany agreed to provide what they had — the manufacturing technology for more than 80 relevant products from 18 of its companies — for China to start its own components manufacturing. This technology transfer was estimated to cost China 140 million yuan.

With the technology support from Eastern Germany, China invested 100 million yuan to establish the Beijing Vacuum Tubes Factory in Jiu Xianqiao, a suburban area northeast of Beijing. It was the largest of its type in the whole of Asia at that time, with an annual output volume of 12.20 million tubes. The location later became the first large-scale electronic industrial park in the early history of China, incorporating large state-owned companies and institutions such as Beijing Electronic Machines Factory, Northern China Wireless Equipment United Factory, Beijing Cable Devices Factory and Northern China Photoelectric Technology Institution.

At the same time, Chinese students studying in Western countries started to return to their motherland and China began to experience an initial boom in its semiconductor industry development. The success of its first monocrystalline silicon under the direction of Lin Lanying in 1959 (only one year after the US), the subsequent success with polycrystalline silicon, the application of its self-developed transistors into the 109 Computer Machine in 1958 and its first integrated circuit made in 1965, proved that China had the determination and capacity to vitalize its electronics industry.

During the 10-year Cultural Revolution starting from 1966, China's semiconductor industry, like all the other sectors, was severely handicapped and halted by the insanity engulfing the country. It was not until 1972, when the US President Richard Nixon made an ice-breaking state visit to China, did the country's semiconductor industry start to seek technology support from the Western world again. In the same year, China's first self-developed PMOS (P-type metal-oxide-semiconductor) LSIC was successfully produced in Yongchuan Semiconductor Institution. Although the pace was rather slow, the achievements were quite impressive.

1. *The Decade After 1966*

Before the turbulent years began in the late 1960s, China kept a close pace with the advanced players in the semiconductor and electronics industry. In the decade after 1966, the gap was lengthened year after year due to the strained political environment both inside and outside the country.

At that time, gathering all of the country's top scientists to carry out research and development work at military and national levels had been successful. There were such extraordinary achievements as atomic and hydrogen bombs and man-made satellites. However, the same strategy would not work if China wanted to make money out of the semiconductors. There seemed no way of achieving an output volume in China that was commercially lucrative as a domestic market and demand did not exist.

Also, the Coordinating Committee for Export Control's restriction on any advanced technologies concerning capitalist countries' national interests and security from being transferred in any form to socialist countries had resulted in China being unable to purchase semiconductor manufacturing equipment and techniques from more advanced companies in the world.

Domestically, the 10-year upheaval in China deformed its social and political structures and twisted the mind of the people and the country. Unrealistic modes of production was propagandized, so much so that the newspaper was full of stories like grandmothers making monocrystalline silicon with their household stoves. The standardized industrial deployment of China's semiconductors had come to a complete halt.

Two bewildering episodes aptly described the situation in China at that time. The two largest factories in China's semiconductor industry, the Eastern Light Electronics in Beijing and the No.19 Factory in Shanghai, were publicly criticized and scorned for its supposed extravagance of layering their factory floor with water polished stone slabs, which was actually a standardized requirement for the manufacturing process. After this incident, factories became unsure and timid to go after quality and innovation.

Another incident happened in 1973 when the China-US relationship resumed and the opportunity to import Western advanced technology beckoned. A program to purchase a production line for color televisions from the US was halted because the Chinese delegation inspecting the US factory accepted glass snail as souvenirs for the visit. The acceptance of the souvenirs by the Chinese inspection group set forth an unexpected and severe political disturbance for the much-needed program. The incident also cost China a rare opportunity to import a full set of IC production line from Japan's NEC.

In contrast, Taiwan imported a 3 inch wafer manufacturing line from the US and started commercial production in 1977. The following year, the Korean Institution of Electronic Technology followed suit and bought a 3 inch wafer production line and put it into operation in 1979. In 1980, Taiwan's United Microelectronics build its first 4 inch wafer foundry factory. For mainland China, it was not until eight years later in 1988 that it had its first 4 inch wafer foundry manufacturing line, established by the Shanghai No. 14 Factory with technology support from the Bell Telephone Company. The lateness was due to a number of reasons and the international export control was clearly one of them.

Despite the turmoil that was happening in China during that period, there was one bright spot that was worth mentioning. It was the successful development of China's first 1024 bit DRAM in the 109 Factory of CAS under the direction of Wang Yangyuan from Peking University in 1975. Although it was not a world-leading achievement, it was still a product that was five years ahead of Korea's semiconductor industry.

China's first 1024 bit DRAM in three different configurations.

During the 1960s and 1970s, due to its fiscal ailment, China's five-year investment plan in its semiconductor industry could not even match the investment amount of a leading US semiconductor company in a single year. In 1973, when China was preparing to purchase the IC manufacturing line from Japan's NEC, it had only a budget about half of the Japanese quotation. During the 1980s, the Chinese government's investment in semiconductors continued to be bogged down by its slack economy and the international export control. Even its strength in DRAM microchips was surpassed by Korea.

2. *Deep Concern from China's Scientists*

Many people felt that since China had been doing well in the industry before the Cultural Revolution, it should not be so difficult to make up for the loss inflicted by the 10-year disaster and bridge up the gap thereafter. However, technological progress could be so revolutionary and disruptive that every step backward would result in a bigger gap to be overcome in the long run.

The decade-long national chaos from the late 1960s stretching into the beginning of the 1980s devastated China's industry facility and scholar society. Its microchip industry was reduced to a rudimentary level, and production was scattered and manual. It was estimated that China lagged 15 years behind the world's leading players in semiconductor research and technology development, and at least 20 years behind with regards to manufacturing capacity. This startling gap had been expanding instead of shrinking over the years, and the catch-up was even more difficult, as the microchip industry was a progressive industry that changed with every passing day and was intertwined and inter-influenced with nearly every other sector.

On the front page of a 5th December 1977 issue of the *People's Daily*, an official newspaper of the Chinese government, there was an article titled *Electronics Industry Leads into Modernization*. The article acknowledged the fundamental importance of the electronics industry in propelling China's modernization process by providing the basic material and technological support. It also admitted the great challenges faced by the country and the big gap between China and the rest of the world including those late-comers like Japan and Korea. While recognizing a series of remarkable achievements made during the 10-year instability, the article encouraged and gave confidence to the whole nation to work together for the future.

The significance and urgency to develop China's own semiconductor industry became a consensus among the government's policy-makers. In the National Science Seminar held in August 1977 in the People's Grand Hall and attended by 30 representatives from China's scientific circles, Wang Shouwu spoke about the overall backwardness of China's semiconductor industry, "The annual output volume of all of China's 600-odd factories combined equals only 1/10 of the monthly output volume of one big factory in Japan." China's scientists were deeply concerned with the wide gap between China and the developed countries in semiconductors and other areas as well. One of them warned that if the situation were to continue, there would be a day when China's young scientists would be discarded by the international scientific society.

Participants of the National Science Seminar held in 1977.

Many policy makers and scholars were not fully aware of the challenges ahead and the efforts required. Once, Wang was asked to bring China's semiconductor industry to the level of developed countries within one year.

5.4 Efforts in the 1980s and 1990s

The reform and opening-up policy initiated by Deng Xiaoping in 1978 greatly emancipated China's production potential across its economic sectors. To infuse new blood into China's semiconductor industry, two programs — to adopt market economy mechanism and to import foreign technologies — were carried out respectively in the 1980s and the 1990s. However, in the end, the policy of "Import, Digest, Absorb and Innovate" did not go far beyond the phase of "import".

1. The 531 Strategy

The year 1980 was the first time China purchased a full set of IC production line from foreign countries. At Wuxi city's Jiang Nan Wireless Devices Factory, an official notice on the billboard announced that the factory had bought a 5 micrometer IC manufacturing line for color and black televisions from the Japanese company Toshiba.

The factory, also called 742 Factory, started in 1960 as a small-scale state-owned factory focused on the production of diodes. It went through several transfers and integrations, and finally came under the leadership of China's Electronics Industry Department. It was responsible for the development of semiconductor techniques and manufacturing of new equipment.

This cooperation with Toshiba made the 742 Factory become China's first IC manufacturer with a modernized industrial production line and operation management. Several years after the imported production line was put into commercial operation, the 742 Factory was able to yield 30 million ICs annually, the biggest output volume among China's IC manufacturers. It was estimated that 40% of China's domestic televisions, stereos and radios used microchips produced in

Jiang Nan Wireless Devices Factory in 1969.

the 742 Factory. This success went on for decades and made Wuxi city one of the strategic bases for China's IC industry.

Despite the success of the 742 Factory, there were many other problems ahead of China's semiconductor industry in the very beginning of a new age. The most crucial ones included repeated import of the same foreign technologies by different Chinese factories and the poor cooperation and integration between different factories and different industrial chains. A report revealed that although 33 state-owned companies bought IC manufacturing lines costing a total of more than 1.3 billion yuan from abroad, only a few of them was put into operation in the end, leaving the rest wasteful and useless.

There was actually a reason for the problem of over-import of technologies. The reform and opening-up policy introduced the market economy mechanism in a hope that enterprises would find their own way under the guidance effect of the market. In doing so, the government hoped that it could cut down its investment on the electronics industry. However, the first reaction of Chinese enterprises, who longed for an immediate return, was to buy technologies and production lines from foreign countries instead of doing research and developing their own technology.

Whether the force of market can push the Chinese microchip industry forward was a question that no one could answer. The key word was *exploration*, just as the State Council's paper in October 1981 put it, "It is like wading through a river without knowing how deep the water is. We must pay attention to every step we take, keep both of our legs in balance and coordination, and make a tentative try before we set forth our foot. It's okay to have taken a wrong step, because that is how we know how to take the right step, as long as we don't allow ourselves to fall over."

One year later in 1982, the Electronic Computer and LSIC Government Work Team was formed under the leadership of Vice Premier Wan Li. Its main task was to work out a development plan for China's semiconductor industry between 1981 and 1985, the 6th five-year-plan, in the fields of electronic computer and LSIC. To address the problems of repeated import of technologies and the lack of integration within the industry, the work team proposed two industry bases and one aerospace center. The southern base was centered around Shanghai, Jiangsu and Zhejiang, the northern base comprised Beijing, Tianjin and Shenyang, and the space center was located in Xi'an.

After years of investigation and preparation, the Electronics Industry Department proposed its first major strategy for the next five-year-plan at the Integrated Circuits Development Strategy Conference held in 1986 in Xiamen. The development plan was named the 531 Strategy, because it involved a nationwide promotion of the 742 Factory's 5 micrometer IC technology, and the development of 3 micrometer and 1 micrometer technologies. The strategy also focused on establishing two or three large and leading factories in China, supporting a dozen of medium-sized enterprises, and leaving room for small-sized companies to participate as well.

With the strategy put into motion, the 742 Factory in Wuxi city was visited by semiconductor companies all over the country. They were there to get a grasp of the 5 micrometer IC manufacturing technology. The factory, being the vanguard of the 5 micrometer promotion move-ment, trained hundreds of technicians for China's IC industry and sent its own engineers to support the operation of other factories.

The technology could be learned from the 742 Factory, but the equipment still needed to be bought from abroad. The following three reasons concluded from the practice of equipment purchasing partly

THE JOURNEY OF CHINA'S MICROCHIPS | 173

explained the gap between China's IC technology and world-leading technology and between China's IC market and the global market.

1. The equipment and production line were bought from different countries and different companies, which resulted in the problem of incompatibility in the later manufacturing process.
2. Little attention was paid to the significance of mastering relevant technology mechanism and management experience in the process of purchasing foreign equipment.
3. Not enough research and development work was in place to spur China's own innovation in the industry. Even the leader of the industry, the 742 Factory did not develop its own core technology and had to buy 2–3 micrometer techniques and production lines from Toshiba and Siemens, and 0.9 micrometer production line from Lucent Tech in the US.

Apart from the above factors, there were also financial problems. The originally planned three microelectronic bases in Beijing, Shanghai and Wuxi required an investment of 400, 500 and 600 million yuan respectively. Due to difficulties in raising enough money, the project was postponed and the Beijing base was suspended in the end.

Despite all that, the main target of the 531 Strategy was achieved. By the year 1988, China's annual IC output volume reached the threshold of 100 million, a number indicating that its semiconductor industry had realized mass production. This process took China 23 years, starting from 1965 when its first integrated circuit was successfully made. In contrast, the US arrived at mass production level as early as 1966 and Japan followed suit two years later. In this sense, the policy of "Import, Digest, Absorb and Innovate" actually did not go far beyond "import", otherwise the 531 Strategy would have been more successful.

2. The 908 Project

For the next five-year-plan of its semiconductor development, China decided to carry out a project that was aimed to realize the 1-micrometer manufacturing technique. The project was called the 908 Project because it was officially announced in a conference held in August 1990, and it was directed by the National Development Plan Committee and the Electronics Industry Department.

The key protagonist of the project was Wuxi Huajing Microelectronics Corporation, derived from Wuxi Microelectronics United Corporation which consisted of the manufacturing capacity of the 742 Factory and the research capacity of the No. 24 Electronics Institution. The company was the first of its kind to be equipped with a 2–3 micrometer production line. It was the industrial leader and was responsible for the output of more than 500 electronics engineers, researchers and leaders in management ranks.

The production line of Wuxi Huajing Microelectronics Corporation.

The 908 Project allotted 3/4 of its total investment fund of 2 billion yuan to Huajing Microelectronics to establish a wafer foundry with a monthly output volume of 120,000. The rest of the investment was given to nine semiconductor companies to set up their design centers. Expectation was high for this project to narrow the gap between China and the world's leading industrial standard.

The outcome, however, turned out to be rather disappointing. It was not until seven years after the project was first implemented that Huajing Microelectronics was able to start mass production. The

THE JOURNEY OF CHINA'S MICROCHIPS | 175

approval procedures for related financial applications took two years, the purchase and installation of Lucent's 0.9 micrometer technique took three years, and the construction work for the factory took two years. With the passage of these seven years, Huajing's 0.9 micrometer manufacturing technique was already 4–5 generations behind the world's mainstream standard when it began to yield output in 1997. Furthermore, the envisaged 120,000 monthly output proved to be unrealistic because the actual number was only 800. This serious deviation from the original plan resulted in a loss of 240 billion yuan in the first year of Huajing's commercial operation.

At this difficult time, Huajing's cooperation with Central Semiconductor Corporation from Hong Kong saved it from impending failure. In February 1998, Huajing leased part of its manufacturing equipment to Central Semiconductor, and the latter put it into profitable operation within five months with a fund of US$28 million, technologies purchased from the US and personnel hired from Taiwan. One year later, Huajing and Central Semiconductor merged to establish a joint venture — Wuxi Huajing Central Semiconductor Corporation, which quickly became mainland China's first merchant foundry factory.

In retrospect, the 908 Project was yet another exploration that tried to lead China into the market economy. The transition from planned economy to market economy was not as simple as the changing of a word; it involved the fundamental change of entrenched mindsets, intertwined operation modes and the wisdom to take it slowly without clashing against existent interests. In market-economy Singapore, where a semiconductor development plan was taking place at the same time, it only took three years from the execution of initial planning to the realization of mass production and five years to make profit. The 908 Project was a failed exploration.

5.5 The 909 Project

After the failure of the 908 Project, it was decided in 1995's Premier Conference that China was going to invest 10 billion yuan, five times the investment in the 908 Project, to establish its 8 inch wafer foundry with 0.5 micrometer and even more advanced manufacturing techniques.

It was a do-or-die mission, fueled by a shocking sense of crisis after a government delegation's visit to a Samsung factory. Hu Liqi, Minister of the Electronics Industry Department, recorded the events of the project in his book. He said, "The government leaders were so determined and resolute to catch up with the manufacturing capacity of the developed world in semiconductors that they were ready for China to exert its last resource to achieve that."

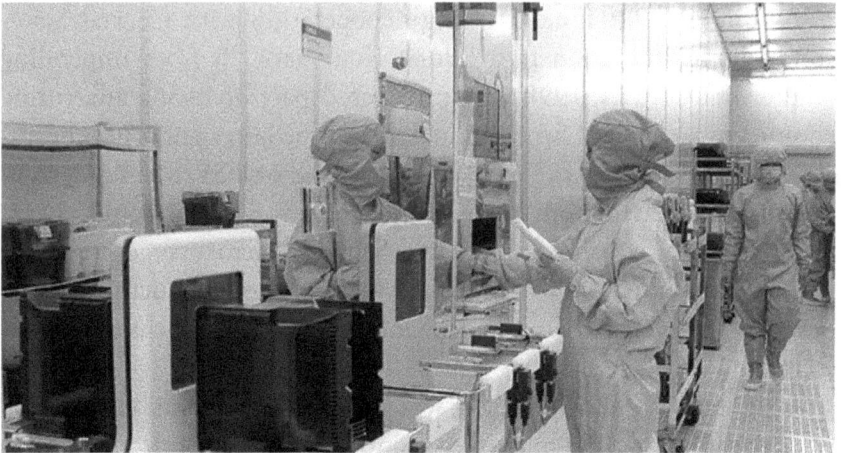

The 8 inch wafer production line in Huajing.

1. *Lessons Drawn from the 908 Project*

There was indeed a sense of crisis in China's semiconductor industry in terms of industry scale and technology standard. Statistics from 1994 revealed that mainland China's combined IC output volume and sales volume amounted to only 1/3 of the capacity of TSMC, a single company in Taiwan, and constituted merely 0.3% and 0.2% of the world capacity. About 85% of China's domestic market share was flooded by imported microchips, and China's manufacturing standard still remained at a level of 4–5 inches and 2–3 micrometers, which was 15 years or 3 generations behind the US and Japan.

This huge gap cost China a great deal of economic benefits as well as an opportunity to climb up the industrial ladder to gain momentum and resources for further development. By 1994, China became a leading color television manufacturer with an annual output volume of hundreds of millions. The profit, however, was meager because the main proportion of returns came from the microchips, and the patents, technologies and designs related to them. China was seriously lagging in all of these areas.

A report in the mid-1990s submitted by the Electronics Industry Department warned that China was in acute shortage of key technologies that could earn foreign countries' cooperation and communication. It also pointed out candidly that China risked being trapped in a position as an electronics assembly line if it failed to develop its own strength in semiconductors. However, whether China could bridge the gap was determined not only by extraordinary efforts, but also by opportunity and global atmosphere. The stake was high, yet the attempt needed to be made.

Therefore, a call for a more daring and more realistic project was made, and the experiences and lessons drawn from the previous 908 Project would be a great help. In his book, Hu recalled the problems revealed in the 908 Project and the challenges faced by the 909 Project, which was discussed in the Premier Conference he attended at the end of 1995. The procedure issue had taken two years for the 908 Project and it could not be allowed to happen again. With a doubling in IC integration and performance every 18 months, semiconductor was one of the fastest changing industries. Such rapid growth also meant a rapid phase-out of what used to be advanced. Time, therefore, was valuable more than ever. That was why the conference decided to made it easy for the 909 Project procedures and to spent precious time on where it was needed the most. Another lesson from the 908 Project was to let the market function as a guide and an incentive for companies, whether established or new ones, to decide on product positioning and capital flow.

2. Unforeseen Challenges and Barriers

As the project rolled out, new companies were founded one after another, with more advanced technologies, more scientific management and more powerful financial support. Among them, Huahong Semiconductor Cooperation shouldered most of the expectations of the project. Unlike Huajing's seven years of slow work, Huahong was put into mass production about one and half a year after its preparation began in July 1997, achieving a sales volume of 3 billion yuan and a net profit of 516 million yuan in 2000. The company's 64 megabyte and 128 megabyte SDRAM microchips produced with 0.35–0.24 micrometer technique were acknowledged by the international market. Whether Huahong's products could successfully gain market share and whether it could succeed in embarking on a virtuous cycle of generating profits would determine whether the project was successful. In 2005, the last year of the 2001–2005 five-year plan, Huahong realized all the goals and met the expectations set for it at the beginning of the project. According to statistics from 2017, the company was the world's 9th largest merchant wafer foundry.

Huahong-NEC headquarters in Shanghai.

As far as the final results were concerned, the 909 Project was successful. Moreover, new practices and policies were doing a good job supporting the follow-up programs aimed to bring out further potential of China's semiconductor industry. Hoewever, the project also revealed some unforeseen barriers and challenges, for example, the unforeseen market instability and price volatility. As China was able to confront this problem early, it became a valuable experience for future solutions.

Another key issue faced by China's semiconductor industry during this time was where to find its place in the world market, or in more ambitious terms, where to make its breakthrough in order to win more market share. It was clear even then that the global market for semiconductors had already been taken up by a few leading companies who were not only able to make reliable and sound products with their mature and advanced technologies, but also able to scale down the manufacturing costs and make more profits. It was bound to be a hard fight with them in order to win over their market share in an environment of intrinsic instability and volatility. It was like trying to hop onto a fast-moving high-speed train, where timing, jumping speed and landing point all mattered to the success.

Hu summarized in his book three good advices for the future development of China's semiconductor industry.

1. A company should lay out concrete measures and long-term planning for re-innovation when it decided to import any form of foreign technologies, and should see to it that they were executed. Import should serve as a means of self-development and self-improvement instead of self-contentment. Most of the cases, however, key technologies should never ever be imported in any form.
2. A company should be market-oriented in choosing which technology was worth importing. New and advanced should not be the main criteria, which should rather be whether it could yield returns from the market.
3. A company should always regard its R&D personnel as its most precious asset and its driving force for innovation.

References

1. Huang Kun & Max Born. *Dynamical Theory of Crystal Lattices* [M]. Beijing: Peking University Press. 1989.

2. Huang Kun & Xie Xide. *Semiconductor Physics* [M]. Beijing: Science Press. 2018.
3. Huang Kun. *Solid-State Physics* [M]. Beijing: Peking University Press. 2014.
4. Zhu Yiwei. *The Last 50 Years of IC Industry* [M]. Beijing: Electronics Industry Press. 2016.
5. Chen Chenjiang & Yu Lisheng. *In Commemoration of Huang Kun*. Beijing: Peking University Press. 2008.
6. Li Yanping, Kang Jing & Yin Xiaodong. *A Biography of Wang Shouwu*. China Science and Technology Press. 2015.
7. Hua Liangfu & Wang Shouwu. *60 Years Persistence in Developing China's Semiconductors* [J]. Innovation Time. 2015.
8. Li Yanping & Wang Shouwu. *China's Achievement in Semiconductors* [J]. China Science Daily. 2014.
9. Wang Zengfan. *A Biography of Xie Xide* [M]. Golden Wall Press. 2008.
10. Ni Sijie. *Doctor Xia Peisu, A Lifelong Legend* [N]. China Science Daily. 2014.
11. Zheng Guoxian. *A Biography of Lin Lanying* [M]. Writers Publishing House. 2005.
12. Hu Qili. *A Memoir on the 909 Project* [M]. Beijing: Electronics Industry Press. 2006.
13. Zheng Shilong, Chen Zhixin & Tian Jingying. *From Jiang Nan Wireless Devices Factory to Huajing* [J]. Outlook. 1986.

Chapter 6

China's Series of Breakthroughs

Overture

Despite all the "big gap" talk, we should be careful not to look down on China's ability and capacity in semiconductors, because the country has its own strengths in particular areas of the industry.

Looking into the mirror of history can always help to illuminate the future. China must be strategic in its quest and bid for the overlap of the technology curve and the market demand curve in order to catch up and surpass the leading technology.

Given that big data is disrupting the traditional R&D of semiconductors and training of application scenarios is increasingly propelling the advancement of chips, there are good reasons to think that China will make breakthroughs in the yet-to-be mature global AI ecosystems.

> I gaze afar on land long lost in the northwest,
> Alas! I see but mountain crest on mountain crest.
> Blue mountains can't stop water flowing;
> Eastward the river keeps on going.
>
> — *Buddhist Dancers, Written on the Wall of Zaokou, Jiangxi,*
> by Xin Qiji

6.1 Is China Lagging Behind in the Global Semiconductor Industry?

In section 2.2.2, we raised the question of why China's rapidly growing high-tech industry did not manage to produce core technologies of adequate competitiveness and deterrence, and what was behind the development bottleneck in China's semiconductor industry. We gave a brief summary of the three long-standing challenges that existed and continued to exist in China's extended efforts to shake off its dependency on Western semiconductors. The challenges were long-term heavy investment, accumulated industrial ecosystem and an adequate talent reservoir. In this chapter, we ask readers to think about the answers to these questions by looking back at the successes and failures made by China during the 1990s and thereafter. Looking into the mirror of history can always help to illuminate the future.

Ye Tianchun, the Director of the Institute of Microelectronics at CAS, once likened progresses and breakthroughs in the field of science to advances in mountaineering. He believed that the area of integrated circuit was by far the highest and the most dangerous mountain, akin to the Himalayas, to be climbed by human beings, and core microchips was like Mount Everest. China might have conquered Mount Tai, Mount Hua and the Alps, but the most daunting height was Mount Everest.

Ni Guangnan, a Chinese Computer Association's Lifetime Achievement Award winner, said that we should be careful not to look down on China's ability and capacity in semiconductors, because the country has its own strengths in particular areas of the industry. For example, in HPC area, China's self-developed microchips have been at the top of the world since 2016. As for smartphone microchips, Chinese companies like Huawei is now at the same level as world-leading companies. In other areas, such as computer CPUs, there is still a 5-year lag in China's capacity. The gap is even bigger in communication semiconductors, and it is here that China still depends heavily on foreign components due to inadequate investment in the area from an early stage.

China's top position in HPC semiconductors is a result of its long-term planning. As one of the symbols of its national science standard,

HPCs play a fundamental role in China's security maintenance, nuclear weapon development and aerospace research. That is why the race among developed countries to develop faster, stronger and more compatible HPCs never stops.

China was determined to develop its own HPC back in the 1990s when the American government put a strict export restriction on the selling of hi-tech products to China. Besides setting an extremely high price for its HPC exported to China, the US also put down rules to restrict its accessibility after it arrived in China. The supercomputer had to be placed in a transparent glass room; the key had to be kept and every time China wanted to use it, it had to produce an application and a statement. This had been a very frustrating experience for China. In 1992, China's self-developed Galaxy-2 HPC was born, which was followed one year later by the Dawning 1. In 2008, China's HPCs entered the Top 100 list in the world, which was dominated by US HPCs made by a group of scholars from American universities. The thrilling news came in June 2011 when Tianhe-1A HPC was ranked at the top of the list, and Tianhe-2 took up the number one position for the following four years.

Despite the top rankings, China's HPC nonetheless relied on microchips designed and made by Intel. In 2015, the US DOC forbid US companies from selling HPC microchips to China for the updating of the Tianhe series under an alleged concern that the microchips might be used by China to conduct nuclear weapons research.

In 2016, China released the Sunway TaihuLight HPC installed with its self-developed Sunway CPU microchips produced by Shanghai High Performance Integrated Circuit Design Center with the top-notch technology of open source framework. China finally achieved self-dependency in its HPC microchips. The Sunway TaihuLight HPC again took the top position of the list and surprised the rest of the world, especially the US who tried to block China's progress in HPC by imposing export control. Furthermore, China's HPCs, represented by the Tianhe, Sunway and Dawning series, accounted for a larger proportion of the world's Top 500 list than the US.

Notably, HPC's concurrent computation system is not as demanding as CPU's single-core performance in the area of server and desktop

Scientists inspecting Tianhe-2 HPC in National HPC Center in Guangzhou.

computer. Moreover, the independent operation system adopted in HPC does not need to be compatible with Microsoft's Windows system, which is also a different story in the server and computer area. These two reasons are why Chinese companies might take some more years to catch up with the world's leading players in the field of computer and server CPUs.

How can China ensure that its core information infrastructure is able to achieve an independent and secure innovation? Ni outlined three core standards for defining independent and secure CPU in April 2018 after the ZTE incident.

1. The developer institution meets China's requirement for confidentiality and security;
2. The instruction system is able to achieve a continuous self-improvement;
3. The kernel source code is written independently by China itself.

Ever since the beginning of the 21st century, China has invested in a series of efforts aimed at the world market for server and computer

Ni Guangnan outlined three core standards for defining independent and secure CPU.

CPUs, including the development of CPU microchips from Ark, Loongson, Sunway, Feiteng and PKUnity.

Loongson microchips are predominantly applied in China's self-developed Beidou Navigation Satellite System, the world's fourth global navigation system. Loongon is steadily building up its own industrial ecosystem by focusing on developing its own technologies from the very beginning. The company's CEO Hu Weiwu laid out the company strategy as designing and tailoring self-developed CPU for specific applications, as he knew his company could not count on foreign capital and technology to realize self-dependency and that recognition from the market for specialized products was crucial for the trial-and-error process.

Unlike the independent development mode of Loongson, Unigroup resorts to acquisition to attain necessary technologies for further development. After taking control of Yangtze Memory Technologies (YMTC), China's leading memory design and manufacturing company,

Unigroup invested a total of US$100 billion to memory chips and devices manufacturing factories. This marked its first step to dominate China's memory chips market.

According to an official statement from Unigroup, YMTC successfully developed the 14 nanometer 64 gigabyte memory chips, one of China's semiconductor achievements that could be considered as world's leading technology. The 14 nanometer project cost an investment of more than US$1 billion and took a period of two years. What if the company instead invested heavily in CPUs instead? Could the efforts in CPUs succeed too? No was the answer from Unigroup's CEO Zhao Weiguo, who knew very well that Intel was too powerful in the field of server and computer CPU microchips to be reckoned with.

Happily, when it comes to smartphone microchips, China can have the confidence to hold its head up high. Huawei Hisilicon, as China's strongest and largest smartphone microchip designer, recently released new products of its Kirin series microchips which were advanced enough to compete with the products of leaders like Qualcomm and Samsung. In the list of 2017 World's Top 10 Fabless Manufacturers (companies who design and sell hardware devices and semiconductor chips while outsourcing the fabrication process, as contrasted with semiconductor foundries like TSMC from Taiwan and SMIC from mainland China), Qualcomm was ranked at number one and Hisilicon with its US$4.7 billion sales volume was ranked at number seven.

Hisilicon's remarkable and proud achievement was a result of Huawei's long term investment, which amounted to a total of 394 billion yuan during the 10 years from 2008 to 2017. In the list of global enterprises' investment in R&D in 2017 released by the European Commission, Huawei was placed at world's No. 6 and China's No. 1 with its €10.4 billion annual investment. Huawei's rotating CEO Xu Zhijun announced that in the following 10 years, the company would continue to invest about 15% of its annual sales volume into the R&D section to fuel future development.

As the world's foremost large-scale communication equipment manufacturer, Huawei also invests heavily in the development of communication microchips. There are as many different types of microchips working in a communication base station as there are many different tasks in communication signals, emission, reception, filtration, stabilization, amplification, analyzing, processing, transmitting and distributing, all of which require specific functionalities of different microchips. This complexity is why China's telecommunications semiconductor companies find it hard to realize self-dependency in the area.

6.2 The Ark and Loongson Attempts

China celebrated a series of exciting triumphs at the beginning of the 21st century, such as Beijing being selected to host the 2008 Olympic Games, China being accepted into WTO after many rounds of setbacks, and the Chinese football team playing in the World Cup for the first time in history. These thrills at the millennium were complemented by new efforts in China's semiconductor industry, represented by an independent and invested R&D on CPUs. Ark and Loongson microchips were the pioneers in China's efforts to get out of its dependency on foreign suppliers. The path to success was strewn with thorns, as usual.

1. *The Ark That Was Gone*

Ni, an academician of more than 70 years in the CAS, the developer of China's first self-designed vacuum tubes computer (Machine 119) and the first person to introduce the association function into the Chinese Pinyin input method, was devoted to China's semiconductor cause. He advocated independent development of core technologies which he believed should start with microchips designing. His aspiration was for China to have a company as dominating in the industry as Intel, and his plan to establish a joint-venture integrated circuit designing center together with Fudan University and Yangtze Computer Corporation was an initial step towards that. The plan got the support of the CAS and the Electronics Industry Department, who invited the participation of other semiconductor companies to form a national investment program and appointed Lenovo as the coordinator of the program.

From a private-level plan to a national investment program, the prospect for the project seemed optimistic. However, Ni and Liu Chuanzhi, the founder of Lenovo, were at odds with each other when it came to the emphasis and positioning of the program. The former wanted to pursue technological breakthroughs regardless of the immediate market reward. The latter, as a successful entrepreneur, strongly opposed that and was determined to act on market effect. In the end, neither of them could persuade each other and the two parted ways, with the program suspended.

After leaving Lenovo, Ni continued to stick to his blueprint of developing China's own CPU and operation system, which involved numerous R&D work that could not generate outright profit. In 1999, Ni and the Ark Technology decided to work together. The company had been doing outsourcing manufacturing in semiconductors for Motorola and Hitachi for quite some time. It was bogged down by a business crisis and was looking for someone to help it emerge out of its crisis. Ni was impressed by Ark Technology's mature personnel and CPU manufacturing technology, which were exactly what he needed to realize his all-time aspiration.

An engineer who had worked under Ni described his obsession towards developing core technology as a scientist's vision, a foresight of what would be at stake in the future. Ni pinned the hope of establishing China's Intel on his cooperation with Ark Technology. He endeavored to enlist as many support and resources as he could. He proposed a strategy to use self-developed CPU installed with the Linux operation system to replace the prevailing Wintel system, and by doing so he hoped to take a slice of the domestic market.

In April 2001, the Ark-1 CPU was released. Though still premature in some key technology parameters, the self-developed CPU received huge attention and all-round support in China. Its technology accreditation committee consisted of academicians from the CAE and was chaired by the former director and vice director of the CAE. It was launched in a glitzy event organized by the Information Department and the Industrial Department. The Beijing municipal government placed an order to buy thousands of network computers installed with the Ark-1 CPU.

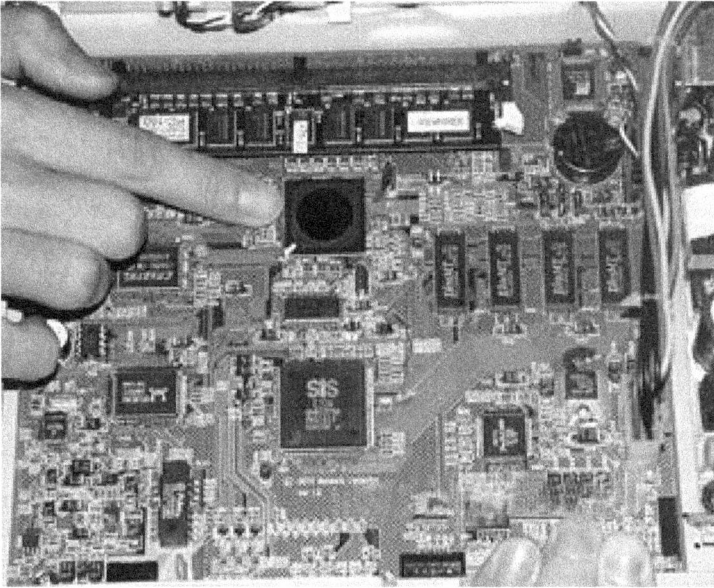

The Ark-1 CPU.

The prospect for the new Ark computers seemed bright, but there were many problems as well. For example, software in the Ark system was incompatible with most of the software in the market, the ubiquitous loopholes in a first-generation product, users were unable to open the files they received, more than 50 bugs existed across 13 categories of applications, etc. As complaints poured in, demands for a switch back to Wintel system spread across the country. A government institution even hired specialized people from universities to make a defect appraisal report on Ark network computers as a support for rejecting purchases.

Years later, when Ni's assistant recalled what happened with the Ark CPU, he mentioned one critical reason for its failure in the market, which was a lack of awareness for user experience. At the end of 2003, the government started to remove Ark network computers from its purchase list, resulting in a sales downturn in Ark-1 CPU. Ark Technology Corporation announced that they would halt follow-up R&D efforts on the Ark CPU despite the support of the 863 Program from the government.

Ni never gave up and still fought for support to upgrade the Ark CPU in 2006, as he was disappointed that the 1.0 version never got the chance to be updated into a better 2.0 version. He believed that failure in the market did not mean failure in the technology, because everyone who participated in the development process had grown to be a better technician and every barrier which was crossed would contribute to a new technology. The important thing was to keep the accumulation process going and not to give up midway because of inevitable defects.

2. *Loongson's Success in Beidou Navigation Satellite System*

Ni's perseverance in technology was admirable, but the evolution of Chinese computer chips from 1.0 to 2.0 would be intrinsically propelled by the ecosystem of the microchip industry, or the force of the market. China finally realized this after a long time and after a series of failures and losses. Some semiconductor leaders understood early on that a grasp on the market was as important as technology. This was something that Chinese microchip developers had not been able to figure out.

Work on the Loongson chip, also known as the Dragon chip, began in 2001 at the ICT, and became a cornerstone of the national high-tech R&D program embarked upon since 1986. From technology development to product and service transformation and to market recognition, the Loongson team had gone through several rounds of painstaking efforts in each generation of the Loongson CPUs. The most challenging part came not from the big gap in technology level, nor the inadequacy of development fund, but from the under-developed market ecosystem.

Loongson-1 CPU, Loongson-2 CPU and Loongson-3 CPU (from left to right).

The concept of an ecosystem in the semiconductor industry is very important. The collaboration between Intel and Microsoft, together with numerous software and hardware, has constituted an ecosystem that has dominated the PC industry for more than 30 years. Other electronics giants, including Apple and Google, have also established their own ecosystems within the industry. That is why they can boast about their dominance while Loongson is still working hard to provide its specific value to the market in an attempt to establish its own ecosystem.

An article written by Christopher Mims in *Wired* in 2009 asked readers to "imagine that your nation is entirely dependent on a belligerent and economically unstable foreign country for precious commodity. Imagine that without that commodity, your entire society would grind to a halt. Imagine that your nation is China, the belligerent nation is the US and the commodity is CPUs."

Mims predicted the outbreak of conflict between China and the US in 2017. He said, "China is also deeply reluctant to build military hardware on top of Western processors, and if that sounds paranoid, keep in mind that there is concern in Washington over whether the US military should use American designed chips that have merely been manufactured overseas. Given those issues, it's not hard to understand why the Chinese government sponsored an ambitious initiative to create a sort of national processor."

This ambitious national processor is the Loongson chip. Although outsiders had the impression that an enormous national investment (1.5 billion yuan was disbursed to Huajing alone in the 908 Program) was spent on the Loongson project, it received altogether only several hundred million yuan since 2001. At the beginning of the project, the research team led by Hu Weiwu was granted 1 million yuan by the ICT to develop a prototype for the Loongson CPU. The team applied for another 10 million yuan as a startup capital for the Loongson Project.

This tight investment forced Hu to cut down on costs as well as to shorten the research cycle by extending the working hours of his research personnel. They volunteered to work six days every week and more than 12 hours every day without extra pay for a few years when the research program was under way. For this reason, Hu felt incredibly indebted to his colleagues for their sacrifice and attributed every progress made in Loongson to their contribution.

Analysts were optimistic that Loongson chips could usher in an era of post-Windows PCs with a lower cost. However, in order to encourage adoption of its processor, a new operation system as well as software need to be developed or adapted for the Loongson chip. Will Loongson-powered PCs make inroads with the average consumer in the world?

In 2013, 11 years after the first Loongson chip was released, Hu decided to focus on the development of specific-purpose microchips in areas like space exploration, intelligence gathering, industrialization, encryption and international commerce. From computer CPUs to market sectors where the industrial ecosystem was easier to establish and technological advantage was quicker to form, Loongson chip took up a strong position in the market of purpose-built microchips. It was doing especially well in the sector of space exploration, as witnessed in the wide application of its chips in China's Beidou Navigation Satellite System. Thanks to this targeted adjustment in the market, Loongson's sales volume has seen steady growth since the latter half of 2014.

Loongson's journey is not just about the completion of a series of products; it is also about the establishment of a market ecosystem with its own software and hardware. Only through the setting up of an independent and secure technology ecosystem of both software and hardware can a company really have a say in the industry and expect a constant self-improvement in the industry.

Another lesson drawn from Loongson's experience for China's semiconductor breakthrough is that the ultimate goal for developing a new technology or product should be based on the demand of the market and on the judgment of whether it can help to dominate the industrial system in the long run.

6.3 Huawei's Perseverance in Hisilicon

Why is Huawei, one of China's two largest telecoms equipment manufacturers (the other one being ZTE), seemingly indefatigable in the face of relentless US pressure? One of the main reasons behind Huawei's tenacity is Hisilicon, a semiconductor designing company fully owned by Huawei itself. Over the last 20 years, Hisilicon has developed eight generations of Kirin CPUs that evolved from being discarded by the market to leading the industry. It is this self-dependency on core microchip products that give Huawei the confidence to defend itself against external attacks.

In 1991, four years after the establishment of Huawei, and three years before the turning-point development of its C&C08 digital-controlled switch machine, Huawei founded its Application Specific Integrated Circuit Design Center amid a time of uncertainty. With this, Huawei embarked on a long journey to realize self-dependency in microchip development. Two years later, the design center developed the company's first digital application-specific integrated circuit.

By the year 2004, Huawei had grown into China's leading semiconductor company with a sales volume of 46 billion yuan and thousands of employees. It was time to invest more into its microchip design center. In the same year, Hisilicon ("Hi" stands for Huawei) Semiconductor Corporation was founded in Shenzhen to pave the way for Huawei to realize its innovations in its chipset solutions. Now, Huawei has become a world leading fabless semiconductor and IC design company, whose chipsets and solutions in high speed communications, smart devices, applications for AI and IoT, and data centers have been proven and certified in more than 100 countries and regions in the world.

Logo of Hisilicon.

In 2009, Hisilicon launched its first smartphone CPU, the K3 into the market. The product was targeted at low-end knockoff digital devices, but failed to be welcomed by the market due to a number of functional flaws that needed to be corrected. In 2012, Hisilicon released

K3V2, on which Huawei built its flagship smartphones. One year later, the first of Huawei's Kirin series CPU, the Kirin 910 was released. It was an ARM-based quad core SoC for Android smartphones and tablets, mostly used in Huawei's own models. The SoC integrated four cores and a memory controller, which were responsible for processing most of the instructions and data, and a LTE Cat radio responsible for internet connection. As Hisilicon's first SoC, Kirin 910's performance in the market was less than satisfactory, but it heralded an era of truly self-developed CPU for Chinese companies.

Less than one year after Kirin 910, a new generation of Kirin CPU was developed and adopted into Huawei's new flagship smartphones. The response from the market was encouraging. Ever since then, a series of new Kirin CPUs has been launched and gained increasingly stronger positions in market share and customer satisfaction. The latest Kirin 980 is the world's first 7 nanometer processor mobile AI chipset.

In the evolution process of the Kirin series, Huawei's financial support and purchase orders played a paramount role in providing trial-and-error opportunities for the CPU series to realize prompt upgrading. Huawei's persistent investment in Hisilicon helped the IC design company to power through those uncertain beginning days when no company would place an order. Huawei also pushed itself towards a new height when many thought the US attack was far too devastating to withstand. Ren Zhengfei, the founder and CEO of Huawei, always insisted upon self-reliant innovation. He believed that no company could survive and see tomorrow without it.

Huawei's investment in innovation is one of the highest in the world, amounting to 15% of its annual revenue. However, Huawei's bold move to boost Hisilicon's capacity for self-upgrade in the early stage by building its smartphones and other smart devices on the primitive Kirin series required courage and vision, because a premature CPU could mean risks and failures for the final devices, as was seen in the example of the Ark computers.

Huawei's risk-taking venture in Hisilicon is based on an understanding of the market. With all the previous lessons, Chinese companies are now well aware of the role of the market in determining whether and when to develop and commercialize new technology. As China's biggest semiconductor company, Huawei has to develop its own microchips technology in spite of all odds, as its eyes are set on a larger market share and a bigger economic return. Self-dependency in microchip design means less licensing fees paid to other semiconductor giants, and more reliable and controllable supply of core microchips.

Hisilicon microchip.

6.4 China's Fight Back in Supercomputers

Dawning, the name of China's first self-developed supercomputer, means "the beginning of a new era", as explained by Li Guojie, the chief architect of the HPC.

In 1993, the Dawning-1 Supercomputer was launched under the famous high-tech research program, the 863 Program. On the 3rd day after the HPC's release, the US lifted its export control of HPCs below 1000 MIPS to China. Wang Daheng, the chief advocator and designer of the 863 Program, proclaimed that the success of Dawning-1 was as valuable to China's science development as the Two Bombs One Satellite Project.

The Dawning-1 ushered in an era where China no longer needed to depend on the mercy of a few Western countries in order to buy their unwanted, low-end supercomputers and use them under strict supervision. China's HPCs were no longer forsaken for their slow operation speed.

With an investment of 2 million yuan and a day-and-night work schedule of a group of scientists led by Li, the 640 MIPS Dawning-1 was successfully developed within one year. With a performance far better than the imported HPCs, Dawning-1 achieved a series of breakthroughs in symmetrical system structure and core codes operation system.

The Dawning-1 HPC.

1. *The Marketization of The Dawning Series*

Although it had a much lower price compared with foreign supercomputers, only three first-generation Dawning series HPC were sold across the whole of China. The newly-developed supercomputer met with barriers, including incompatibility with international mainstream operation systems and software applications.

The following years were spent on solving the problem of incompatibility. Not long after, researchers started to develop Dawning's own operation system and to enhance the reliability and maintenance of the machine. After years of trial and error, the Dawning series finally dominated China's domestic market for a consecutive four years. It entered the list of the world's Top 10 supercomputers in 2012 for the first time.

Dawning's headquarters in Beijing.

2. *Sunway TaihuLight, the Champion of Supercomputers*

Liang Jun, the vice director of the National Research Center of Parallel Computer Engineering and Technology, admitted that many Chinese were unsure if the country should continue to invest heavily in self-developed CPUs despite all these years of setbacks and failures. Some of them questioned whether it was sensible and necessary to spend continuous effort to establish China's own industrial ecosystem in semiconductors. The achievements realized in China's Sunway TaihuLight HPC, however, once again proved that it was of vital importance to attain self-dependency and self-sustainability in the industry.

In a room with an area of 1,000 square meters in the National Supercomputer Center in Wuxi city, there is a supercomputer spread out across 48 equipment cabinets, each the size of a double-door refrigerator.

In every one of these cabinets, there are 1,024 Chinese-designed 64 bit processors based on Sunway architecture. This is the Sunway TaihuLight, translated as "divine power, the light of Taihu Lake". Running at a rate of 93 petaflops, the supercomputer was twice ranked first in the Top 500 list from June 2018.

The Sunway TaihuLight HPC.

Yang Guangwen, the director of the Wuxi Supercomputer Center, explained the computing capacity of Sunway TaihuLight in layman's terms, "Each of the 40,960 processors can work as 20 personal computers, and the work done by the whole system in the room in one minute would take the planet's 7.2 billion population 32 years to finish without rest or sleep." There are many applications for such powerful supercomputers, for example, simulating the origin and evolution of the universe and life, calculating the precise trajectory of space crafts, and singling out effective medicine through molecule chemical technique, etc. Supercomputers are indispensable in fields of high-end material science and bioscience and also in deep sea exploration and space exploration, where there are large amounts of calculations. It is fair to describe supercomputers as the base that supports a giant pyramid.

Each of the Sunway Taihulight's processor contains 256 processing cores and an additional four cores for system management, all running on Sunway's own operating system. China is now investing around 3 billion yuan to develop its first exascale supercomputer, which is expected to enter service by 2020.

6.5 Unigroup's Successes in Acquisitions

The semiconductor industry is a highly divided yet integrated ecosystem in which no single entity can prosper on its own. Even industry leaders like Intel and Qualcomm need to depend on intellectual properties and patents of ARM, which provides technology structure for 95% of the world's smartphones and tablets. Some companies pay huge amounts of license fees for access to indispensable technology developed by others. Some companies own them once and for all through acquisitions, like Unigroup. This proved to be an efficient way to stand on the shoulders of former giants.

On 8th May 2018, Tsinghua Unigroup, China's top microchip designing company, went public on the A-stock market. Market analysts linked Unigroup's move to another round of capital operations. After all, the company was known for its successful and rewarding acquisitions of four influential semiconductor companies in the field. These purchases enabled the group to become the most vital entity to help China build a competitive semiconductor ecosystem and cut the heavy reliance on foreign suppliers.

Beijing-based Tsinghua Unigroup is a subsidiary of Tsinghua Holdings. Established in 1988, it is a manufacturer of wireless systems-on-chip and radio frequency semiconductors for cellular, connectivity, and broadcast applications. The company's products are incorporated into mobile handsets, set-top boxes and other wireless and consumer electronic devices.

Several years ago, Tsinghua Unigroup bought and privatized Spreadtrum Communications and RDA Microelectronics, two Chinese mobile chip makers that were originally listed on Nasdaq. The acquisitions, valued at US$1.78 billion and US$907 million respectively, made Unigroup the third largest smartphone chip fabless company in

Unigroup's headquarters.

the world. Its later acquisition of Yangtze Memory Technology and more than US$100 billion investment in memory chip manufacturing were viewed as China's hope to eventually challenge top global NAND flash memory chipmakers such as Samsung Electronics and Toshiba. Furthermore, Unigroup spent US$2.5 billion to replace HP as H3C's main shareholder. In the process, it became China's largest and world's second largest internet products and service provider.

In 2014, Intel invested US$1.5 billion for a 20% stake in Unigroup. A recent collaboration with Intel would see Unigroup being supplied wth Intel's 5G modem chips in the second half of 2019. Unigroup would be able to bundle Intel's 5G modem with its own application processors and provide a total solution chipset to clients. Such a deal would give Unigroup an opportunity to close gaps with its bigger rivals.

Unigroup's chipsets could be found in Samsung's entry-level handsets, Chinese smartphone made by Lenovo Group and TCL as well as Indian phone brands like Lava and Micromax. The company's global market share in providing mobile processor chips was 11% in 2017, compared with 36% for Qualcomm and 24% for MediaTek.

Unigroup-designed SDRAM.

6.6 China's AI Chips Are Poised to Take the Lead

In April 2017, CAS set aside 10 million yuan (US$1.4 million) to develop a brain-inspired processor chip specialized for deep learning. Called Cambricon, the chip was the world's first processor that could simulate human nerve cells and synapses to conduct deep learning.

Cambricon was named after the Cambrian explosion, a sudden flowering of a great diversity of new life forms that began roughly 540 million years ago. The Cambricon research project was helmed by brothers Chen Yunji and Chen Tianshi, who were two of the youngest full professors at the ICT and whose aspiration was to enable machines to better understand and serve humanity. In 2015, Chen Yunji was selected as one of *MIT Technology Review*'s 35 Innovators Under 35. Younger brother Chen Tianshi was Founder and CEO of Cambricon Technologies, a company set up in March 2016 to bring the Cambricon chips to market.

The two brothers were responsible for the basic research on architectures and algorithms for the Cambricon system. Unlike existing neural networks like AlphaGo which require thousands of GPU-based accelerators, Cambricon processors were designed to operate more efficiently and run on much less power. According to an announcement made at the 3rd World Internet Conference held in China in 2016, the Cambricon-1A chip could handle 16 billion virtual neurons per second

Chen Yunji and Chen Tianshi (from left to right).

and had a peak capacity of two trillion synapses per second. This performance was double that of a conventional GPU (graphic processing unit) but had a power consumption lower by one order of magnitude. Huawei's Kirin 970 chip, which was used to develop its Mate-10 smartphone, utilized Cambricon's intellectual property.

Aiming to have one billion smart devices using its AI processor and capture 30% of China's high-performance AI chip market within three years, Cambricon Technologies launched another three AI processor IP products in November 2017, all of which involved substantial evolvement of the Cambricon-1A chip. The Cambricon-1H8 focused on lower power consumption, providing up to 2.3 times performance per watt over the Cambricon-1A chip. The Cambricon-1H16 had wider application and better performance. The Cambricon-1M was made for intelligent driving and had 10 times the performance of Cambricon-1A.

The company said that the three new AI processors could be applied to image recognition, intelligent driving, security monitoring, unmanned planes, automatic speech recognition, natural language and other applications. In May 2018, the company launched high performance machine learning processor chips Cambricon-MLU100 and Cambricon-MLU200 for servers and an AI software platform Cambricon NeuWare for developers.

Cambricon-MLU100 high performance deep learning processor.

Cambricon Technologies is now one of the highest-valued smart chip startups in the world. Its Series B funding round in June 2018 saw its valuation soar to US$2.5 billion. Investors reportedly included several Chinese state-owned companies, government-supported Capital Investment Group and industry leaders like TCL, Alibaba and Lenovo. Its previous investors included iFlyTek, Oriza and Yonghua. iFlyTek is a voice recognition company and part of China's national AI team, while Oriza and Yonghu are early-stage investment companies with a technology focus.

Cambricon's ambitious target is in line with the Chinese government's stated goal of building a 1 trillion yuan (US$152.5 billion) AI core industry by 2030, supported by domestically designed AI processors that can rival US companies like Intel, Qualcomm and Nvidia. The AI semiconductor industry is yet to be matured enough to form a developed industrial ecosystem around the world. There are several countries who are eager to lead the industry by establishing an ecosystem pivoted on their own interests. Statistics showed that from 2015 to 2017, worldwide investments in AI chips rose from US$800 million to US$1.6 billion, the number of companies focused on developing AI chips went from just a few to more than 20, and the latter half of 2017 saw more than 30 different AI chips waiting to be mass produced in TSMC's manufacturing line. With this development trend, it was estimated that by the year 2025, the market of AI chip would reach a value of US$12.2 billion on a compound annual growth rate of 40%.

This is an opportunity for Cambricon and China to pursue a leading role in the global ecosystem on the same starting line as Nvidia, Intel, Google, Facebook and Microsoft, all of whom are active in developing deep learning microchips. China has the world's largest market, is a step ahead in its AI chip development, and has an efficient industrial network of companies in all AI sectors. From both technology and finance perspectives, the country looks to be a very promising candidate to lead the international AI ecosystem, and Cambricon will no doubt be the impetus for China to achieve this dream.

6.7 BAT: New Builders of Microchips Ecosystem

After the US banned American firms from selling chips and other components to the Chinese telecoms company ZTE for seven years, Chinese e-commerce giant Alibaba announced the acquisition of Hangzhou C-SKY Microsystems, one of the leading Chinese microchip makers. This was a clear and targeted move to boost Alibaba's cloud-based IoT business and to enhance development of its own chip capacity.

Founded in 2001, Hangzhou-based C-SKY Microsystems develops embedded CPU and chip architecture based on the IPs it purchased from Motorola. According to the company, it is the only embedded CPU volume provider in China with its own instruction set architecture. C-SKY Microsystems has already developed seven types of embedded CPUs which cover a wide range of embedded applications, including smart devices in IoT, digital audio and video, information security, network and communications, industrial control and automotive electronics. In 2017 alone, the company picked up 70 licensees in China. By the end of 2018, more than 700 million SoC chips based on C-SKY architecture had been shipped.

Alibaba had previously invested in Hangzhou C-SKY Microsystems and now its stake in the company is 100%. This move is in line with

Alibaba's interest in chips which play a significant role in empowering and incorporating different industries through the e-commerce titan's cloud-based IoT solutions. It also underlines the company's commitment to drive the development of China's chip industry after the ZTE incident, which triggered a heated discussion concerning the necessity for self-sufficient tech supply chains in China.

The acquisition seems to be successful and beneficial for Alibaba, which has reportedly started developing a neural network chip for image analysis and machine learning called Ali-NPU in the Alibaba DAMO Academy (The Academy for Discovery, Adventure, Momentum and Outlook). The chip is designed for image recognition, video recognition and cloud computing to improve overall computing power and to reduce manufacturing and operating cost. According to Alibaba, the purchase of C-SKY Microsystems will help unify the two companies' R&D capabilities amid China's ongoing campaign to gain self-reliance in key technologies.

Alibaba is set up in 1999 by Jack Ma, a former English teacher from Hangzhou, China. The company's primary goal is to champion small businesses, in the belief that the internet would level the playing field by enabling small enterprises to leverage innovation and technology to grow and compete more effectively in domestic and global economies. Today, Alibaba is the world's largest retailer and e-commerce company, one of the largest internet and AI companies, one of the largest venture capital firms, and one of the largest investment corporations in the world. It is named as one of the world's most admired companies and one of the world's top 10 most valuable enterprises by *Fortune*. Today, using AI technology, Alibaba is still devoted to powering the future of business.

The chips will be part of Alibaba's ambitious plan to deliver AI through cloud computing and IoT devices. The company is already using AI to improve online shopping and process city data. Using in-house chips will help it do things faster and more cheaply.

AI chips are at the heart of the future trend of digitalization and intelligentization of nearly every aspect in social and business scenarios from auto-driving cars, IoT to robotics. AI is expected to transform economies. It has been called a "winner takes all" technology, meaning that companies and countries that gain an edge will build upon that lead over time. "Artificial intelligence is the future for all humankind," said Russian President Vladimir Putin. "It comes with colossal opportunities, but also threats that are difficult to predict. Whoever becomes the leader in this sphere will become the ruler of the world."

In America, leading companies like Google, Apple and Facebook as well as many startups are designing their own AI chips and buying up chip companies with a goal to design chips that fit their businesses. There has also been a recent push by Chinese firms and researchers to do the same. Baidu, Alibaba and Tencent, the three largest internet companies in China and also known as BAT, have come to realize that the huge returns brought about by an innovative commercial mode has long ended, and that the new engine for future breakthroughs definitely hinges on leading the semiconductor technology.

China's government has unveiled a three-step development plan to steadily build up its AI capabilities from 2020 to 2025 and to lead the world by 2030.

Building up an AI engineering talent pool is the key to the plan. Chinese scholars are already producing AI research papers at a faster pace; patents in robotics and other areas have also soared. Chinese internet companies have set up their AI research centers in Silicon Valley and other critical parts of the world. The BAT and other hi-tech companies are paying top salaries to snag AI scientists from all over the world.

Artificial intelligence involves computer algorithms — software programs that aim to mimic the human ability to learn, interpret patterns and make predictions. China's huge population will generate massive big data to train AI systems in how to make predictions. So, there is good reason to think China will make breakthroughs in developing these computer algorithms.

Besides computing power, which is part of the basic infrastructure underlying AI, the BAT is also actively commanding stronger control over the supply of core technologies by investing heavily in microchips development. By building a new ecosystem of software and hardware,

China can potentially leap forward to a leading position in the yet-to-be mature AI ecosystems. Looking back in history, we know that a new industrial ecosystem will emerge and mature in such fast-evolving fashion that we should not waste time pondering what should or should not be done. It is a now-or-never opportunity for China and it is a new epoch for a new leader to write its own history.

References

1. Mei Hong & Qian Yueliang. *On the 30th Anniversary of the 863 National Program*. Science Press. 2017.
2. Li Guojie. *In Quest of Innovation* [M]. Electronics Industry Press. 2008.
3. Tian Tao & Wu Chunbo. *Will Huawei Be the Next Fallen One: A Story, Philosophy and Huawei's Rise and Fall* [M]. China Critic Press. 2017.
4. Liang Ning. *The History of China's Self-developed Microchips and Operation System*. 2018.
5. Hu Weiwu. *The Journey of Loongson-1 Microchip*. 2002.
6. Christopher Mims. *People's Processor: Embrace China's Homegrown Computer Chips* [J]. Wired. 2009.

www.ingramcontent.com/pod-product-compliance
Lightning Source LLC
Chambersburg PA
CBHW071741270326
41928CB00013B/2755